THE MOST DANGEROUS MOMENT OF THE WAR

Japan's Attack on the Indian Ocean, 1942

John Clancy

CASEMATE
uk

Oxford & Philadelphia

Published in Great Britain and
the United States of America in 2015 by
CASEMATE PUBLISHERS
10 Hythe Bridge Street, Oxford OX1 2EW, UK
and
1950 Lawrence Road, Havertown, PA 19083, USA

Hardcover Edition: ISBN 978-1-61200-334-4
Digital Edition: ISBN 978-1-61200-335-1

A CIP record for this book is available from the British Library

Printed in the United Kingdom by Short Run Press, Exeter

For a complete list of Casemate titles, please contact:

CASEMATE PUBLISHERS (UK)
Telephone (01865) 241249
Fax (01865) 794449
Email: casemate-uk@casematepublishers.co.uk
www.casematepublishers.co.uk

CASEMATE PUBLISHERS (US)
Telephone (610) 853-9131
Fax (610) 853-9146
Email: casemate@casematepublishing.com
www.casematepublishing.com

Charlie Clancy   *Geoff Kitchen*

*This book is dedicated to the memory of Charlie Clancy
(1915–2009), a survivor from HMS Cornwall, and Geoff Kitchen
(1923–2011), a survivor from HMS Dorsetshire. Charlie is, of course,
my dad and although I knew about the sinking of these two ships for a
number of years through stories he had told me, it was not until
I met Geoff in 2001, quite by accident whilst on holiday, that I began
to appreciate the full implications of this action.
I am indebted to Geoff for encouraging me to write this book and
giving me free access to his extensive archive. I raise my
hat to both of these gentlemen.*

Contents

Acknowledgements

The front cover picture is taken from a painting by Terence Cuneo CVO OBE RGI (1907–1996). Entitled *Aircraft Attack British Battleship*, it was originally painted for the Ministry of Information during the Second World War whilst Cuneo was serving as a Sapper but he also worked for the War Artists' Advisory Committee, providing illustrations of aircraft factories and wartime events. Cuneo was an eclectic painter and after the war was commissioned to produce a series of works illustrating railways, bridges and locomotives, but a significant point in his career was his appointment as official artist for the Coronation of Queen Elizabeth II, which brought his name before the public worldwide. He received more commissions from industry, covering manufacturing, mineral extraction and road building, including the M1 motorway. He was famous for his passion for engineering subjects, particularly locomotives and the railway as a whole, but in fact Cuneo painted over a wide range of subjects, from big game in Africa to landscapes. Further success was achieved in his regimental commissions, battle scenes and incidents as well as portraits, including Field Marshall Montgomery. In recognition of the respect people have for Cuneo, a 1.5-times life-size bronze memorial statue of him, by Philip Jackson, stands in the main concourse at London's Waterloo Station. It was commissioned by the Terence Cuneo Memorial Trust, established in March 2002, as a permanent memorial to the artist. The Trust also provides an annual prize at the Slade School of Art, Cuneo's former school.

It is sometimes difficult for writers to produce an accurate picture of past events, particularly when trying to assess how the people involved discharged their duties and responsibilities, when they themselves were not present. I myself fall into this category but I think my training as an archaeologist will stand me in good stead, for I am used to researching a subject, gathering together all the available evidence, the facts and the figures, from a number of different sources, and piecing it together coherently, rather like a jigsaw puzzle. The only thing we cannot say with any certainty is why certain people did what they did at the time. To know this you would need to be inside that person's mind because not even he who stood next to that person would truthfully be able to say. We can only offer our best guess based on the evidence before us, which is what archaeologists are particularly adept at. For this reason I have drawn to some extent on the works of other writers whose books appear in the section headed 'Further Reading' and I take this opportunity to acknowledge them.

This book is dedicated to the memory of all of those who took part in these operations in the Indian Ocean and Ceylon between March and May 1942, especially those who were killed in action. And whether you approve or not, for I know many will not, we cannot fail to extend this tribute to the enormous efficiency and fighting spirit of the Japanese forces who opposed us, despite them sometimes being guilty of barbaric acts of treatment towards their prisoners, but then that is a fundamental part of their militaristic culture and code of conduct. But it is no excuse for their flagrant disregard of the Geneva Convention.

Every effort has been made to authenticate the information received from various sources but sometimes time can play tricks on the memory so if any part of my text is inaccurate I sincerely apologise and will endeavour to correct it in any future editions of this book. Every reasonable effort has been made to trace and acknowledge the copyright holders of the pictures used herein but should there be any errors or omissions or people whom I could not contact, I will be pleased to insert the appropriate acknowledgement in any future editions.

John Clancy, BA (Hons), MA

Introduction

War in the Far East erupted with the most spectacular and successful bombing raid ever seen; that fateful day at Pearl Harbour on 7th December 1941 will live on in the annals of infamy. Over the next eighteen months results almost as spectacular were claimed, but nothing compared with the attack on Pearl Harbour. Even though the Americans had good reasons for expecting the attack, given that war between Japan and the United States had been a possibility of which each nation had been aware (and developed contingency plans for) since the 1920s, the enormous surprise which the Japanese managed to achieve was totally unexpected, even by their own pilots, so when these same airmen came to attack Ceylon some four months later, the British, despite having extremely accurate and comprehensive intelligence of Japanese intentions, were taken only a little less by surprise.

Without wishing to appear to be overstating the events that took place in and around Ceylon, or Sri Lanka, in March and April 1942 too highly, such was its extent and magnitude it could so easily have become known as 'Pearl Harbour, Part II'. To the Japanese it was known simply as Operation C, a naval sortie by their fast aircraft carrier strike force under the command of Vice-Admiral Chuichi Nagumo against Allied shipping and bases in the Indian Ocean in an attempt to force the Allies to retreat to East Africa, thus leaving the Japanese unopposed in the Indian Ocean.

Ceylon remembers it as 'The April Raids'; Sir Winston Churchill later described it as being 'so dangerous to our cause'; and the historian, Sir Arthur Bryant said, 'A Japanese naval victory in April 1942 would have given Japan total control of the Indian Ocean, isolated the Middle East and brought down the Churchill government'. It was a situation aggravated by the possibility that at the same time the Germans could have captured Egypt and closed our routes to the Middle East. It is all too easy to overlook the gravity of these events or to underrate the concern that prevailed as the Japanese swept westwards, brushing aside any opposition. There seemed to be no holding them back and in early April 1942 over a thousand lives, mostly British, were lost as the Japanese made their only major offensive of World War II westwards. It has even been questioned why a film has never been made about this incident because like the attack on Pearl Harbour, it has all the necessary ingredients to become a blockbuster.

But what made Japan decide to carry out such an unprovoked and cold-blooded attack, especially against a nation with whom she was not at war? Furthermore, once the attack had ended what happened next? Did the Japanese force return from whence it came or did it move on to another target?

In answer to the above questions, the attack on Pearl Harbour was a defiant gesture against America who had imposed unacceptable trade sanctions and embargoes upon Japan in an effort to curb her expansionism. It was also intended as a preventive action in order to keep the US Pacific Fleet from interfering with military actions Japan was planning in Southeast Asia against the overseas territories of Britain, the Netherlands and the United States. Having eliminated the threat of reprisal by the Americans in the attack, the Japanese knew that Britain could be called upon to help so their fleet, based in Ceylon, now known as Sri Lanka, also had to be eliminated or at least driven out of the Indian Ocean. But as well as keeping the Japanese at bay, the British also had an on-going secondary challenge to deal with, political unrest amongst the indigenous populations of Ceylon and India who were demanding Home Rule and Independence, so this too is factored into the story.

This book will therefore, bring to light a little-known chapter of World War II, an early engagement of the Pacific campaign that seems to have escaped narration, except in a fleeting way by only a few authors.

As will be seen in the following chapters, this was to be a war like no other. In a very short space of time battle tactics had to be re-thought and altered according to unfolding events because the beginning of the Second World War marked the end of the battleship as the dominant force in the world's navies. Large fleets of them, many inherited from the Dreadnought era decades before, had until now been one of the decisive forces in naval thinking, but by the end of the war battleship construction was all but halted, and almost every existing battleship was retired or scrapped. Its obsolescence was brought about by the newly discovered offensive power of the aircraft carrier. The sinking of the British battleship *HMS Prince of Wales* and her escort, the battle cruiser *HMS Repulse*, confirmed the vulnerability of a battleship to air attack, in this case while at sea without air cover. It ably demonstrated that even the most modern battleships could not defend themselves against an aerial attack without proper aerial defences, and in turn it led to a new technique of aerial combat against ships in which in a well-planned attack, fighter planes strafed the battleship to suppress the AA guns while dive bombers used their armour-piercing bombs to cause topside damage and havoc. But these fighters and dive bombers were merely diversions to allow the delivery of aerial torpedoes.

During the early years of the war, from 1939 to 1941, the battleship still dominated naval warfare, and there were several battleship versus battleship actions across the Atlantic and Mediterranean theatres, albeit in some cases with decisive intervention by aircraft carriers (such as against the *Bismarck* and at Cape Matapan, Greece). Indeed, the Battle of Cape Matapan (27–29th March, 1941) was to be the Royal Navy's last fleet action of the twentieth century. Some farsighted commanders even suggested the aircraft carrier would become the capital ship of the future and during the Pacific War, aircraft carriers did take precedence with there being just two engagements in which battleships fought each other.

As Japan began hostilities it became evident the situation in the Indian Ocean would drastically change. The rapid advance of the Japanese army and the presence of a large Imperial naval force in the South China Sea meant the Allied naval force in that area would either have to be increased in size or completely withdrawn to the coast of

The main armament of *HMS Repulse*, totally useless against an attack by aircraft.

East Africa. Following the fall of Singapore and the sinking of the *Prince of Wales* and the *Repulse* the Japanese High Command was in agreement that of these two options, the British Admiralty would soon move a fleet into the Indian Ocean using Ceylon as its base, so a plan of attack was prepared. Early in March, Admiral Yamamoto issued the order to attack and destroy enemy forces around Ceylon during the period from mid-March to the beginning of April. This attack was to include a raid on the Bay of Bengal to destroy all British merchant shipping there because as well as the practical objective of bringing to a standstill seaborne commerce to and from the east coast ports of India, it also posed a psychological threat to our forces in Calcutta, thus weakening their effect on the Burma campaign. It came at a time when all British military strength was committed to saving Burma.

As the collapse of Burma continued, the Admiralty was well aware of the danger to its Eastern Fleet and was resigned to the fact the Japanese would probably be making another carrier-based raid similar to the attack on Pearl Harbour. But despite recognizing the danger they were in, the Admiralty could do little about it. The Royal Navy was already hard-pressed on so many different fronts that it had hardly enough ships to cover any of them. Nevertheless, the Eastern Fleet had to be strengthened so that it could maintain control of Ceylon because without it, essential convoys from India to Europe and the Western Desert in Africa would be in constant danger.

The Japanese plan was to leave their base at Kendari on the south-east peninsular of the Celebes (now known as Sulawesi) in Indonesia on 21st March and attack Ceylon on 1st April with the aim of achieving a similar level of surprise to that achieved at Pearl Harbour. Unbeknown to the Japanese however, the US Navy had broken their naval code and it was an outline of this plan that reached Admiral Somerville on 28th March. In spite of this the operation was delayed by the appearance of a US Navy carrier raiding force at Wake Island on 10th March which delayed the Japanese departure until 26th March, the day that Admiral Somerville took command of the newly assembled Eastern Fleet. The attack on Ceylon was therefore delayed until 4th April but the Allies were not aware of this change in the plan which as will be seen, had a critical effect on the outcome.

Following their invasion of the Philippines, Malaya, Hong Kong and Singapore, the Japanese had a vast new coastline to defend, stretching from New Guinea to Northern Burma. Having destroyed much of the American fleet at Pearl Harbour, they could not tolerate the threat posed by the British Eastern Fleet based at Ceylon, so they steamed westward, unopposed, to attack and destroy it in accordance with their master plan. Had they been successful, the Japanese would have gained total control of the southern oceans, a perfect springboard for an invasion of India. So far the Japanese had suffered no significant losses and their offensive continued unabated. It was generally felt Ceylon would be next to fall; as Ceylon held much of the British Empire's resources, particularly of rubber it was a situation that could not be allowed to happen, but the question on everyone's lips was how soon Japan would take advantage of this strategic situation. It was a real threat; no one in history had ever conquered so much territory in such a short space of time and the Allied naval strength in the Far

East was at a dangerously low level. It was Churchill's nightmare of the 'Most Dangerous Moment of the War'.

Plans to strike westwards into the Indian Ocean and take Ceylon had been prepared by the staff of the Japanese Combined Fleet who also envisaged taking Madagascar. Since the attack on Pearl Harbour there had been many meetings between Vice-Admiral Nomura, the Japanese Naval Attaché in Berlin and Admiral Fricke, Chief of Staff of Germany's Maritime Warfare Command (*Seekriegsleitung*), who did much to persuade the Japanese to initiate operations that would assist and support Germany's own efforts against Britain. These talks were mainly to discuss the delimitation of respective operational areas of the German and Japanese navies but at a subsequent meeting on 27th March 1942, Fricke stressed the importance of the Indian Ocean to the Axis powers and expressed the desire that the Japanese begin operations against the northern Indian Ocean sea routes. Fricke further emphasized that Ceylon, the Seychelles and Madagascar should have a higher priority for the Axis navies than operations against Australia. The German Naval Attaché in Tokyo had even provided the Japanese with particulars of suitable landing sites in Ceylon. By 8th April, the Japanese delegation told Fricke they intended to send four or five submarines and two auxiliary cruisers for operations in the western Indian Ocean between Aden and the Cape, but they refused to disclose their plans for operations against Madagascar and Ceylon, only reiterating their commitment to operations in that area.

If Japan's objective was to gain control of the Indian Ocean by destroying Britain's Eastern Fleet, which at the time they thought consisted of two carriers, two battleships, ten cruisers and an unspecified number of destroyers, they might have been better advised to concentrate their ships in just one force. A similar strategy was to prove fatal to them later at the Battle of Midway, but even so, Nagumo's battle fleet was vastly superior to anything he expected to confront and it had the added benefit of three weeks extensive training before setting sail. As he left Kendari, the Japanese base, Nagumo must have been feeling supremely confident of forthcoming success.

In April 1942 Churchill wrote to President Roosevelt outlining the dangers of Japanese dominance resulting in '… the invasion of Eastern India with incalculable consequences to our whole war plan, including the loss of Calcutta and of all contact with the Chinese through Burma. But this is only the beginning. Until we are able to fight a fleet action, there is no reason why the Japanese should not become the dominant force in the western Indian Ocean. This would result in the collapse of our whole position in the Middle East, not only because of the interruption to our convoys to the Middle East, but also because of the interruption to vital oil supplies from Abadan, without which we cannot maintain our position, either at sea or on land in the Indian Ocean area. Supplies to Russia would also be cut as these must go through the Persian Gulf.'

He continued, 'With so much of the weight of Japan being thrown upon us, we have more than we can bear. If you do not feel able to take speedy action which will force Japan to concentrate her forces in the Pacific, the only way out of the immense perils that confront us would seem to be to build up as quickly as possible an ample force of modern capital ships and carriers in the Indian Ocean.'

Churchill later pointed out that the aerial combat in Ceylon had had important strategic results which at the time we could not foresee. Vice-Admiral Nagumo's aircraft carrier force that had earlier devastated the American fleet at Pearl Harbour had ranged almost unchallenged for four months with devastating success but in the raid on Ceylon suffered such significant losses of aircraft, that three of the carriers had to be withdrawn back to Japan for refitting and re-equipping. When a month later Japan launched an attack on Port Moresby in New Guinea, only two of these carriers were able to take part. Their appearance at full strength in the Coral Sea might well have turned the scales against the Americans in that most important encounter.

Britain accepted it was in the Indian Ocean her maritime power would have to be restructured with Ceylon as its main base. It was a policy the Admiralty had originally wanted to adopt but the Foreign Office supported the Prime Minister's view that a small force of fast, modern ships should be based at Singapore. The First Sea Lord eventually agreed to this plan and *HMS Prince of Wales* was despatched to the Far East where she would have been supported by the new aircraft carrier *HMS Indomitable*, only she was put out of action after running aground off Jamaica. It has been suggested this short delay proved fatal to British plans for using Singapore as its base. The plans for *Indomitable* to join the *Prince of Wales* and the *Repulse* in the port of Singapore as part of a deterrent force against Japanese aggression in the Far East, are however, flawed. Given that the *Indomitable* was in the vicinity of Jamaica on 3rd November, 1941, it seems unlikely that she could have reached Singapore in sufficient time to provide air cover for the battle fleet. For that to have been achieved it would have been necessary to order the ship to proceed to Singapore at a much earlier date. Subsequently the other two capital ships did not have adequate air cover and were sunk by Japanese aircraft when the Japanese landed in Malaya in December 1941. In January 1942 *Indomitable* joined the Eastern Fleet at Ceylon from where she ferried 48 RAF aircraft to Singapore during January but these aircraft came too late as the British commanders in Singapore surrendered to the Japanese in February.

With the loss of the *Prince of Wales* and the *Repulse* off the east coast of Malaya, to the north of Singapore on 10th December 1941, the Japanese had virtually undisputed command of the Western Pacific, enabling them to strike at will against the vast and rich territories that were their next objective. From the British perspective, the sinking of these two capital ships had an immediate and disastrous effect on the morale of those defending Malaya and Singapore, as well as shocking much of the rest of the world. It totally shattered the long-held belief in British invincibility. In Ceylon, there was understandably considerable anxiety that a Japanese attack appeared to be both inevitable and imminent, but what form would it take, an invasion or an air raid. As the awareness of the superiority of aircraft carriers over battleships dramatically increased, the fate of all our territories in south-east Asia was clearly sealed. Rarely can a defeat at sea have had such far-reaching consequences.

Speaking of these events after the war in March 1946 when Sir Winston Churchill was the chief guest at a dinner held at the British

Embassy in Washington, he was asked what he thought had been the most dangerous and the most distressing moment of the war. Some thought he would suggest the perceived German invasion of Britain in June/July 1940; others thought it might be when Rommel was heading at full speed for Alexandria and Cairo; and some thought it might equally be the fall of Singapore to the Japanese. None of these incidents sprang to Churchill's mind as his listeners tensely awaited his reply. After a moment's thought he declared without any shadow of a doubt, the most dangerous moment of the war, the one that caused him the greatest alarm and concern was when he received the news that the Japanese fleet was heading for Ceylon and the naval base there. 'The capture of Ceylon', he said, 'the consequent control of the Indian Ocean, and the possibility at the same time of a German conquest of Egypt would have closed the ring, and the future would have been bleak'.

Churchill went on to explain how we were saved from this potential disaster by the brave actions of a pilot, Squadron Leader L.J. Birchall who spotted the Japanese warships massing some 350 miles from Ceylon, whilst on patrol in his Catalina flying boat. Six Japanese Zero fighter aircraft were sent up to deal with him but before they could shoot him down, Birchall was able to send a brief radio message back to his base, giving the defence forces enough time to prepare for the impending attack and disperse the Allied fleet out to sea. Churchill acknowledged that this pilot had made one of the most important single contributions to our victory and called Birchall the 'Saviour of Ceylon'.

It seems strange that this incident which Churchill deemed to be of such crucial importance should have received such little attention by historians. Even those who have chronicled the war against Japan have made scant reference to it. At the time Churchill regarded this to be 'a turning point in the war', but with the benefit of hindsight we now know that the operations dealt with here, neither hastened defeat nor ultimate victory, or led to irreparable losses or material gains to either side but had this Japanese plan succeeded, it would most certainly have had devastating results and would have altered the course of the war.

CHAPTER 1

The Background to the Conflict

The Second World War in the Far East erupted with the most spectacular and successful, but equally shocking bombing raid ever seen, and at a stroke it became a global conflict. What made the attack on the American fleet at Pearl Harbour so contemptible was that there was no state of war between the United States of America and Japan at the time and there was no indication of the situation being otherwise. In fact Japan and the United States were engaged in negotiations throughout 1941 in an effort to improve relations so that crucial and decisive day at Pearl Harbour on 7th December 1941 will be forever infamous, but it was only a part of Japan's overall well planned strategy which few people know about or appreciate.

Fundamentally, the war in the Pacific was a conflict to seize and defend airfields in an effort to gain superiority over America. The Japanese made gaining and maintaining control of the air as much a requirement in their basic war strategy as they did the destruction of the US Pacific Fleet. At the beginning of the Second World War, the Japanese Navy (or, in the Japanese language, *Nihon Kaigun,* or even *Teikoku Kaigun,* the 'Imperial Navy') was almost certainly the most powerful navy in the world. Its Naval Aviation Corps, consisting of 10 aircraft carriers and 1,500 first class pilots, was the most highly trained and proficient force of its kind. Its 11 (soon to be 12) battleships were among the most powerful in the world and its surface vessels, armed with the superb 24" Type 93 (Long Lance) torpedo, were incomparable night fighters. Whilst seemingly advanced in aerial tactics, Japan entered the war with a narrow aerial doctrine, an insufficient number of aircraft, most of which were of generally poor design (excluding the Mitsubishi A6M2 Zero), too few aircrews and inadequate logistics for a war of attrition. Neither its army nor its naval air arm was prepared for the duration, violence or sophistication of the war to come. Even its short-lived lead in aerial tactics collapsed once the Guadalcanal campaign (August 1942–February 1943) began. A point worth bearing in mind is Japan, unlike many other nations, did not have a dedicated air force as such. Its aviation units were part of the army or navy, and they were not well coordinated with each other. All references to Japanese aviators in the ensuing chapters, therefore, refer to carrier-based navy pilots and their aircraft.

At this time Japan was expanding throughout the whole of the Far East following her invasion of Manchuria and China, resulting in a state of war with Russia driven by rival Imperial ambitions. In 1941 it seemed likely that America would intervene by using her economic strength to stop Japan who depended upon American oil and other imports for her war effort. Had America taken this step it would most definitely have crippled Japan's mighty military machine. Japan needed to hit America hard and it was believed in Tokyo that a devastating attack would deter America from having any influence in the Pacific, thus leaving Japan to do as she pleased. And so, on December 7th 1941, a large bomber force attacked the American Pacific Naval Fleet based at Pearl Harbour in Hawaii where three battleships were sunk and sixteen other ships damaged. Over 120 aircraft were destroyed and 2,400 people were killed, with many more wounded. Fortunately the soon-to-be vital aircraft carriers stationed at Pearl Harbour were all out at sea on manoeuvres and the oil reserves kept there had been drained into underground reservoirs, leading some to believe that the American government knew about the raid in advance but let it go ahead so that the American public would be so angered by it, that when President Roosevelt announced he had declared war on Japan they would openly welcome it. In support of this belief, it is surprising to think that all the aircraft carriers were out to sea at the same time, something that had never happened before, and that all the oil, which would have been such a huge loss, was drained into the safety of underground reservoirs. Those ships that were lost were replaceable and so were the aircraft but the carriers would have been much more difficult to replace. However, this advance-knowledge conspiracy theory is rejected by most mainstream historians.

Today it seems unthinkable that a country as small as Japan would have the audacity to challenge someone as mighty as America but in December 1941 that's exactly what they did. Over the next eighteen months results almost as spectacular were claimed, but until the atomic bombs were dropped on Hiroshima and Nagasaki, nothing compared with the attack on Pearl Harbour. It was launched without any warning or formal declaration of war. Japan had not even consulted her Ally, Germany, before taking the decision to attack. Even though the Americans had good reasons for expecting it, given the sanctions and embargoes they had placed upon Japan, the enormous surprise which the Japanese managed to spring on them was totally unexpected, even coming as a shock for the Japanese pilots themselves. When these same airmen came to attack Ceylon some four months later, despite the British having extremely accurate and comprehensive intelligence of Japanese intentions, we were taken only a little less by surprise, a crucial factor in both attacks. We now know that prior to the attack on Pearl Harbour the Americans had managed to decode Japanese radio messages sent between Tokyo and Japanese embassies abroad, and it was from this we now had accurate knowledge of Japanese intent against Ceylon. The signal decrypts provided the commander of the British Eastern Fleet, Vice Admiral Sir James Somerville with warning of the Japanese attack and he retreated to Addu Atoll in the Maldives, expecting an attack on 1st or 2nd April.

The Japanese attack on Pearl Harbour and that planned for Ceylon were not random attacks but were part of a clever and carefully planned strategy, the tactics for which were learned at the Battle of Taranto in

Italy on the night of 11–12th November 1940 between British Naval forces, under Admiral Andrew Cunningham, and Italian Naval forces, under Admiral Inigo Campioni. In this one engagement the Italian Navy lost half of its fleet of capital ships. The Italians had a battle fleet of six battleships, including two of the Littorio class which had only just been put into service and were among the most powerful vessels in the world, and four of the recently-reconstructed Cavour class. This fleet was considerably more powerful, on paper, than our Mediterranean Fleet, but it had consistently refused to engage in battle.

The significance of this engagement at Taranto was that it was here the Royal Navy launched its first all-aircraft ship-to-ship naval attack in history, using a small number of obsolescent biplane torpedo bombers, like Fairey Albacores, from the aircraft carrier *HMS Illustrious*. The attack struck the battle fleet of the Regia Marina, lying at anchor in the harbour of Taranto, using aerial torpedoes despite the shallow depth of the water in the harbour. The devastation wrought by the British carrier-launched aircraft on the large Italian warships marked the beginning of the rise of the power of naval aviation over the big guns of battleships. According to Admiral Cunningham, "Taranto, and the night of November 11–12th, 1940, should be remembered forever as having shown once and for all that in the Fleet Air Arm, the Navy has its most devastating weapon." It was something the Imperial Japanese Navy Staff was quick to appreciate and master, and it is more than likely they carefully studied the Taranto raid whilst planning the attack on Pearl Harbour because of similar issues with its shallow harbour.

Lt. Cdr. Takeshi Naito, the Japanese assistant naval attaché to Berlin, flew to Taranto to investigate the attack first-hand, and probably wrote a report of his findings, although to date no copy of such a report has ever been found. Naito subsequently had a lengthy conversation with Commander Mitsuo Fuchida about his observations. It was Fuchida, of course, who led the later Japanese attack on Pearl Harbour. Of more significance, perhaps, was a Japanese Military Mission to Italy in May 1941 when Japanese naval officers visited Taranto and had lengthy discussions with their Italian Navy opposite numbers. The Japanese had been working on shallow-water solutions for their aerial torpedoes since early 1939 with various ports, like Manila, Singapore, Vladivostok and Pearl Harbour as the hypothetical targets.

It had already been agreed that Britain's maritime power would have to be restructured in the Indian Ocean with Ceylon as its main base. It was a policy the Admiralty favoured but the Foreign Office supported Churchill's view that instead a small force of fast, modern capital ships should be based at Singapore. It was fortuitous for the Admiralty because on 15th February the Japanese completely over-run Singapore, something that Churchill later described as 'The greatest disaster to British arms which our history affords'. The spotlight therefore turned to Ceylon.

The island of Ceylon was strategically important because it not only commanded the Indian Ocean but controlled access to India, the vital Allied shipping routes to the Middle East and the oilfields of the Persian Gulf. Furthermore, Ceylon held most of the British Empire's resources of rubber. The British base on Ceylon was now the last significant naval base in the Indian Ocean, the next link in the chain west of Singapore. If Ceylon fell not only would operations in the Indian Ocean be compromised but the main supply route to the Mediterranean, running up the east coast of Africa, would be threatened. The threat that the Germans might expand east and link up with the Japanese moving westward would suddenly become very real.

Before hostilities broke out in the Pacific, extensive pre-war planning was centred on Dreadnought battleships left over from World War I. The Royal Navy could not achieve parity with the estimated nine Japanese capital ships in Southeast Asia, since doing so would leave only a handful of ships to use against Germany. This was an age-old concept whereby in every naval engagement until now, battles were fought on the basis of ship versus ship using large calibre guns, and Churchill had, after all, on two separate occasions, been the First Lord of the Admiralty so no one dared to question his evaluation of the situation. However, the fall of Singapore to the Japanese in February 1942, coupled with the newly-found evidence of the superiority of aircraft over battleships, as seen at the Battle of Taranto in November 1940, meant that new policies had to be adopted. And so, with all expediency, aircraft carriers started replacing the ageing battleships as the core of any battle fleet. This was what contributed to Japan's success at Pearl Harbour where fortunately for the Americans their aircraft carriers were at sea at the time, out of danger. But not everyone was in agreement with aircraft carriers replacing conventional battleships. They argued that the aircraft carrier was an unusually vulnerable type of ship in relation to its size. It was said, without cruisers and possibly a battleship or two as escorts and a screen of destroyers, the aircraft carrier was a lightly protected, high priority target, an impossible combination in any war.

The Japanese attack on Pearl Harbour was a considerably larger operation than that at Taranto with six Imperial Japanese fleet carriers, each one carrying an air wing that was more than double the number of aircraft any British carrier had. It resulted in far more devastation, sinking or disabling seven American battleships, and seriously damaging other warships, but this assault on the US Pacific Fleet did not alter the balance of power in the Pacific in the same way that the attack on Taranto did in the Mediterranean Sea. The US Navy was instead forced to radically modernize its thinking and make its aircraft carriers their capital ships in naval warfare planning. Compared with the Italian battleships that were a threat in the narrow confines of the Mediterranean, the US Navy's battleships which survived the Pearl Harbour raid proved to be of limited use in the vast expanse of the Pacific Ocean and thereafter operated primarily as fire support for amphibious landings as they were too slow to escort the carriers.

At the time of the attack on Pearl Harbour our knowledge about the Japanese navy and army, and their air wings was limited, which is surprising, considering Japan had been in conflict with China for four years. Prior to that, Japan had fought Russia in the Russo-Japanese War, 1904–5, a conflict that was said to be "the first great war of the twentieth century", growing out of rival Imperial ambitions of the Russian Empire and the Empire of Japan over Manchuria and Korea. Significantly, at the start of that war Japan was recognized by many

Western nations as being the first Asian army and navy to be organized and equipped on modern lines.

But what was it that brought about Japan's aggressive disposition towards her neighbouring countries as well as Britain and America? Why had she embarked on this suicidal policy of expansionism? To answer this it is necessary to take a brief look at her history which for our purposes began in 1600 with the arrival of the British navigator, Will Adams. From 1641–1853 there were no formal relations between Britain and Japan but in 1854 the first limited Anglo-Japanese Friendship Treaty was signed which, despite an interruption during the Second World War, remains very strong up until the present day. The Anglo-Japanese Alliance of 1902–22 was the first formal agreement of its type to be reached by a Western 'great' power with a non-Caucasian nation and as such, it represented an important milestone diplomatically, strategically and culturally. In 1914 Japan entered World War I as a British Ally under the terms of the Alliance and captured German-occupied Tsingtao in China. They also helped Australia and New Zealand capture archipelagos like the Marshall Islands and the Mariana Islands.

Following World War I, the major naval powers joined a number of pacts, each designed to limit naval armaments by means of an agreed formula which would afford reasonable defence against future aggression and to prevent any one nation from building a fleet to threaten its neighbours. Japan accepted this formula at the Washington Naval Conference of 1921 but it limited her navy to six-tenths of the strength of the British and American fleets. This was, in one sense, propitious because Japan was involved only in the Pacific whereas Britain, and America to a lesser extent, each had a heavy naval presence throughout the world.

In 1930 Japan voiced her dissatisfaction with this limitation at the London Naval Conference and an improvement under the terms of the new London Treaty was offered. Both the American and British governments were facing economic crises at this time and neither had any thoughts or desires about increasing expenditure on armaments.

Japan was only able to increase its allowance of ships because Britain and America were interested only in building theirs up to the pre-arranged limit. Furthermore, it had also been included in the 1921 Washington Treaty that neither Western power would build heavy land defences in Asia, something that was to Japan's advantage as she later swept through Malaysia and Burma.

A review of the treaty obligations was conducted at the Second London Naval Conference in 1935 by which time Japan had set her sights on building a large autonomous empire in eastern Asia. She now sought parity with Britain and America in regard to naval power. The implications were clear. Japan was already deeply involved in Northern China, even though she was not at war, as such, there. America was still unwilling to enter into an arms race with Japan and Britain was more concerned with the threat to European peace from Germany's Adolph Hitler. Both countries considered heavy expenditure on armaments to be political suicide. As a former Secretary for the Navy, Franklin D. Roosevelt recognized more than anyone the threat posed by Japan and could clearly see how it was aimed primarily at the USA. He was fully aware of a feeling of compulsive isolationism gripping a large and significant portion of the American public which could not be ignored and because of this the American reaction to Japan's forceful occupation of Manchuria had been restricted to encouraging the League of Nations, of which the USA itself was not a member, into bringing economic pressure to bear against Japan.

When in early 1936 it was clear that Japan's aims would not be met by negotiations, its delegates withdrew from the London Naval Conference, abrogated the Treaty and declined to make public their future plans. Whilst all others continued to observe the armaments limitations imposed by the new London Naval Treaty, Japan chose to ignore this and continued with its programme of building battleships with guns of a much larger calibre than those who signed the new Treaty whilst successfully concealing the build-up of her fleet from the West. Japan was proud of her new navy at this time, in contrast to Britain and America whose governments sought only peace. It was also noticeable how Japan's political power was very much in the hands of naval and military personnel, something that was disproportionate to the modest influence which service chiefs had in Europe and America.

By 1937 Japan's struggle for domination in China, euphemistically referred to as The China Incident, developed into open warfare. Though never officially declared as such, the Japanese fobbed off diplomatic protests with mildly phrased apologies, vague statements of peaceful intentions and bogus complaints against China. Even though the Japanese refused to acknowledge a state of war existed with China, the Chinese accepted it, referring to it as the War of Resistance Against Japan, the Eight Years' War of Resistance or more simply the War of Resistance. In Japan today, the name Japan–China War is most commonly used because of its perceived objectivity but when the invasion of China began in earnest in July 1937, the Japanese government started using the term The North China Incident, and with the outbreak of the Battle of Shanghai the following month, it was abbreviated to The China Incident. The word "incident" was widely used by Japan as neither country had made a formal declaration of war. Although American opinion on the China Incident was gradually being won over, it was not until the time of the attack on Pearl Harbour that Roosevelt felt compelled to align the USA with Britain in Asia, as in Europe, against the Tripartite Powers of Japan, Italy and Germany. At the outbreak of war in Europe America could no longer ignore the potential threat in the Pacific and responded by re-arming, using the full range of her massive resources, and acknowledged that Britain's involvement with the war in Europe left responsibility for the Pacific almost exclusively in her hands.

Japan wanted to avoid intervention by other countries, particularly Britain and the United States, which were its primary sources of petroleum; the United States was also its biggest supplier of steel. If it was formally acknowledged that the fighting had already escalated to a state of "general war", the US President, Franklin D. Roosevelt would have been legally obliged to impose an embargo on Japan in observance of the US Neutrality Acts. For many years Japan had been dependent upon America for oil, raw materials and other supplies, essential items for any industrial nation, but in July 1940 President Franklin D. Roosevelt was granted powers by Congress restricting the export of all potential war materials and Japan was refused iron, steel, fuel oil, aircraft spares, chemicals and other items. Japan's choices were clear; cease hostilities in China or seek an alternative supplier. Clearly she had to look elsewhere for these essential supplies and Indo-China in Southeast Asia was an ideal choice. In order to preserve the very life of the Empire, Japan had no alternative but to go on the offensive.

A year later, less than six months before the attack on Pearl Harbour, all Japanese assets in the United States, Great Britain and the Netherlands were frozen, and despite Japan retaliating in kind, it was clear she was now being held in a tight economic stranglehold. The United States demanded Japan's complete withdrawal from China in return for relaxing these sanctions. Prince Konoye's moderate government gave consideration to this demand, but War Minister, General Hideki Tojo and the strong military element that supported him would not hear of it. Konoye had no option but to resign and General Tojo assumed the premiership. He had no difficulty in carrying the Emperor and the Cabinet with him, and the decision was made for war unless the Americans would appreciably modify their stand. Negotiations were still in progress in Washington when the first wave of Japanese aircraft struck at Pearl Harbour.

It was all of these factors that conspired to bring Japan to a state of war in 1941 and America became embroiled in a way that Russia had also been drawn into conflict with Japan in 1904 – an unheralded attack on its fleet at Port Arthur in the Tsushima Strait between Korea and Japan without a prior declaration of war having been announced. With Russia having lost its place as Japan's main rival in the east, America became the new adversary and Japan no longer saw Russia as an opponent of her expansion plans in Asia; instead it was America. The USA had made its position perfectly clear by taking such a firm line in backing up its warnings with economic constraints which threatened Japan's future development. Knowing full well she could not align herself against Russia and America, Japan was somewhat relieved to hear of the prospects of a German victory in Russia in November 1941 and it was this that had much to do with the timing of her own offensive actions. With Germany now taking care of Russia, Japan believed that by destroying America's Pacific Fleet, America could be forced into withdrawing her support for Nationalist China, oil and other raw materials could be obtained from the Dutch East Indies, Malaya, Borneo and Burma, while Germany disposed of Britain and Russia as effective forces. This would leave Japan free to continue her subjugation of China.

The key to Japan's success at Pearl Harbour was the extent of her air power, a closely guarded secret from the outside world. Its pilots trained far out at sea where even their own people could not see them and foreign observers saw only what Japan wanted them to see. It was a strategy that was so successful that until the attack on Pearl Harbour, the Americans were completely unaware of the existence of the Zero fighter aircraft that inflicted so much damage. It proved to be one of Japan's best-kept secrets. But it was not just the Americans who were ill-informed. The Royal Air Force knew only of Japan's older German and Italian aircraft which it was implied, we might face. Our lack of intelligence about the Zero was a severe handicap, causing many serious miscalculations regarding range and endurance. The real figures were far in excess of what we had been led to believe and were based on a comparative performance of our own aircraft.

What was so special about the Zero? To give it its full name, the Mitsubishi A6M2 Zero was designated as the Mitsubishi Navy Type 0 Carrier Fighter, and was a fast, well-armed, manoeuvrable aircraft with a high firepower and a long flying range that was no match for our fighters whose pilots being unaware of its high performance, suffered many casualties through adopting the wrong tactics in fighting it. In the hands of a well trained pilot, the Zero was more than a match for either our Sea Hurricane or Wildcat in every aspect except for firepower. In early combat operations, the Zero gained a legendary reputation as a dogfighter, achieving the outstanding kill ratio of 12 to 1, but by mid-1942 a combination of new tactics and the introduction of better equipment enabled the Allied pilots to engage the Zero on generally equal terms. Developed by the Imperial Japanese Navy Air Service and deployed from early 1939, it was the most versatile carrier-based fighter aircraft in the world and played a key role in the Battle of Ceylon.

The reason for our lack of intelligence on this aircraft is not fully known. Having seen the Zero in action against China in the spring of 1940, American newspaper correspondents based in Chungking filed reports on it and in that same year details were also sent to the Air Ministry from other sources in the city. Particulars of the aircraft and its performance were sent to the Far Eastern Combined Bureau in September 1941 for onward transmission to Air Headquarters but it never arrived. In addition to the information on this aircraft, a description of it written in Chinese reached Singapore but what happened next is a matter for conjecture since all records have long been destroyed. It is probable that this report was part of the accumulated mass of files the Intelligence Section set up at Air Headquarters in 1941 had attempted to deal with but as war broke out in the Pacific the report remained undiscovered and unread. This lack of knowledge was to be a severe handicap to the navies and air forces of both America and Great Britain.

In many war-themed films featuring this particular theatre of war, most Japanese aircraft seem to have strange epithets like Zeros, Vals, Kates, etc. The reason for this is because Japanese aircraft are identified by their type and use, prefixed by the last two figures of the year in which they came into operational use according to the Japanese

A Zero fighter aircraft.

calendar, so the year 1940, for example, equates to 2600 and the year 1936 is 2596. The Zero fighter aircraft first used in 1940 was therefore named the Navy Type 0, or Zero, carrier-borne aircraft. It was the Americans who later gave these aircraft code names, a practice soon adopted by all the Allies. Other code names included the Navy Type 96 Attack Bomber known as the "Nell", the Navy Type 97 four-engine Flying Boat was a "Mavis", the Aichi Navy Type 99 dive-bomber was the "Val", the Nakajima Navy Type 97 torpedo bomber was a "Kate" and the Zero, although dubbed the "Zeke", was universally known as the Zero.

As the Americans entered the war with Japan, they bravely stood their ground at Bataan trying their best to fight against overwhelming odds, but after seven days of bitter fighting they had no alternative but to surrender. It was the greatest defeat ever suffered by an American force in the field. At a press conference held later, General MacArthur said: "No army has done so much with so little, and nothing became it more than its last hours of trial and agony".

On the same day that Bataan fell, the Royal Navy was also facing the equal humiliation of being forced to abandon the western Indian Ocean to the Japanese following the sinking of the *Prince of Wales* and the *Repulse*. The brevity of the action and the enormous losses sustained added glory to the Japanese victory and shame to our crushing defeat. In a battle lasting less than two hours, the much boosted, newly constituted Eastern Fleet was destroyed, thus negating a mighty and dangerous fighting unit from any interference in future Japanese campaigns in the Pacific. The whole world, already accustomed to expecting great surprises, was stunned at the news of the battle. Questions were asked demanding an explanation from those responsible, but nevertheless, a valuable lesson had been learned for future actions. It proved beyond any shadow of a doubt the overwhelming superiority of aircraft over battleships and showed how heavy naval units operating close inshore without adequate protection fall easy prey to a well-organised, daring and spirited attack from torpedo-carrying aircraft.

Writing about the fall of Singapore in his book *Footprints in the Sea* Captain Augustus Agar, VC, captain of *HMS Dorsetshire* recalled how following the attack on Pearl Harbour, Japanese troops were simultaneously landed on the Malay Peninsular, Thailand and Hong Kong. The British were unprepared for this, having heeded the advice given by the Foreign Office that if we moved our latest battleship, *HMS Prince of Wales* and a cruiser, *HMS Repulse* to Singapore, their presence would deter the Japanese and give us valuable time in which to complete our preparations. They were wrong, of course but the First Sea Lord had to reluctantly concur with the government Minister. His reluctance was heightened when he learned that the aircraft carrier *HMS Indomitable,* an important part of the deterrent force, had run aground off Port Kingston, Jamaica whilst en route to join the Force at Singapore. She then had to sail to Norfolk, Virginia, USA for repairs and it was to be three months before she finally got to Trincomalee.

Captain Agar was an authority on this matter, having studied the possibilities of a war with Japan whilst at the Navy Staff College in 1928 and again at the War Course in 1934, and on both occasions had contributed to a study of the naval aspect of this problem with particular emphasis on the passage of the British fleet to Singapore, where it was hoped the ships using Singapore as a base would be in a position to give battle to the Japanese fleet. Furthermore, Captain Agar had family connections in Ceylon and Malaya.

A closer study of the problem was made by representatives of all three services at the Imperial Defence College in 1935 with particular emphasis on the air issue. It was unanimously agreed that the key to the defence of Singapore lay in the possession of bases in French Indo-China but as was later seen in July 1941, the Japanese colluded with France's Vichy government and occupied French Indo-China. Although urgently required and requested, no naval or air reinforcements were sent to counter this move.

In 1938 Captain Agar who was then the captain of *HMS Emerald,* took part in combined exercises to test the defences of Singapore and the conclusion reached by all concerned was that it was satisfactory. However, the Senior Air Force Officer (then Air Vice–Marshal Tedder) submitted a strong caveat that this did not include the defence of Malaya which needed additional airfields and air forces to defend the peninsular in co-operation with the Navy.

In July 1940 Captain Agar studied the problem afresh in London with Admiral Tower and a small group of naval captains, at the request of the First Sea Lord. When asked how Singapore could be best defended with what we could spare, the answer was to send the four old R Class battleships to deal with any Japanese invasions, provided they had destroyer escort and air cover, either from a carrier or RAF squadrons operating in Malaya. But it was too little, too late.

Following the sinking of *HMS Prince of Wales* and *HMS Repulse*, together with the fall of Hong Kong and Singapore to the Japanese, Allied naval strength in the Far East was reduced to a dangerously low level. Japan had suffered no significant losses so far and her offensive continued unabated further south and to the west. It became essential therefore to put together a multi-national fleet to stem the Japanese tide. Named the Eastern Striking Force, it was hurriedly put together at Soerabaya in Java at the end of February 1942 and put under the command of the Dutch Rear-Admiral, Karel W.F.M. Doorman. His brief was to delay, even if he could not stop, the Japanese invasion of the Dutch East Indies.

As there were no battleships or aircraft carriers available, the fleet consisted of a number of cruisers and destroyers from four different nations. The cruiser *De Ruyter* was chosen as the flagship of the fleet. Other cruisers included the Dutch *Java* and *Tromp*, the British *Exeter*,

HMS Prince of Wales.

the American *Houston* and the Australian *Perth* and *Hobart*. Britain had two light cruisers, the *Danae* and the *Dragon*. Amongst the destroyers were the British *Electra, Encounter, Scout, Tenedos* and *Jupiter*, the Dutch *Kortenaer, Evertsen, van Ghent, Banckert* and the *de With* and the American *John D. Edwards, Alden, John D. Ford, Edsall, Stewart, Parrott, Pillsbury* and *Paul Jones*. Some of these vessels were not an actual part of the Eastern Striking Force but they were involved in the ensuing and slightly earlier operations in the Java Sea.

As can be imagined, the fleet had many disadvantages, the least of which was difficulties in communications. It had no capital ships or air cover, and there had been no opportunity for it to operate together as one cohesive unit. Despite this, the fleet put to sea in the afternoon and night of 27th February and was very nearly overwhelmed by superior Japanese forces that had the advantage of numerous supporting aircraft both by day and by night. By the effective use of flares, the Japanese pilots were able to see every change of course the ships made, so evasion was impossible.

It was a battle which Churchill described as 'this forlorn battle'. It certainly was a humiliating defeat and when over, the last remnants of the fleet, the *Hobart* and most of the American destroyers limped southwards to the relative safety of Australia. Only one Dutch vessel, the *Tromp*, survived, together with the two British light cruisers and two of its destroyers, and they all headed for Ceylon. The Allied casualty rate was high and it included Rear-Admiral Doorman. The survivors were cast up on various islands. The Indian Ocean was now wide open and undefended.

Having taken Singapore and with the support of a large well-balanced fleet, Japan could choose in which direction to move next. Although Japan's motives for entering the war were fundamentally expansionism, she was more interested in Eastern Asia than the Pacific but it was there that the American presence had first to be eliminated. With the Americans still holding out in the Philippines, the Australians defending New Guinea and Malaya having already fallen to the Japanese, it looked likely it would be Burma next.

In support of this, the Japanese invaded two undefended islands in March 1942, the Andaman and the Nicobar Islands, but this was to be their last westwards occupation. They based a detachment of 13 long-range flying boats at Port Blair in the Andamans and felt reassured they could safely reinforce their troops in Burma by sea to Rangoon, which the British had evacuated two weeks earlier. The patrols undertaken by these flying boats proved to be of great value during the ensuing two weeks from 23rd March.

At one point it was thought the Japanese might head for Australia but after much thought and consideration Ceylon and the Indian Ocean generally seemed a more likely target. Four days after the 'Fall of Singapore' the Japanese did venture into Australia, attacking Port Darwin where like Colombo, its harbour was full of merchant ships. Twelve were sunk and many others were damaged to varying degrees. Possession of Ceylon would bring the Japanese to the very threshold of India but first they needed to consolidate their gains in Malaya, Singapore and the Java Sea, giving us an estimated six weeks in which to assemble an Allied fleet. Five battleships and three aircraft carriers were hastily dispatched to Ceylon to guard the sea approaches to India and protect the shipping routes to Burma. It was not exactly a well-balanced fleet but it was a strong force of ships. But what was the Japanese secret that seemed to make them so invincible?

Japanese tactics were both ingenious and simple; it was centred on the skilful use of its air force. Keeping details of the performance of the Zero a carefully guarded secret had paid handsome dividends. Ever since bomber aircraft had been devised in World War One a great deal of thought had been given to developing an accurate method of delivering bombs, especially against moving targets without subjecting the aircraft to enormous losses. Although fighter aircraft could disrupt an attack at virtually any altitude, it was not difficult to fly above the effective range of anti-aircraft gunfire, and it was not always possible to ensure the accuracy required for a bomb drop. When dropped, a bomb tends to fall at the same speed and trajectory as the aircraft dropping it, so even at the highest levels the aircraft might well have travelled two or three miles between releasing the bomb and it hitting its target. A moving target, such as a ship, has only to alter course by a few degrees to avoid a hit. If however the attack is by a large number of bombers attacking from different directions, it is not so easy to avoid.

As the war progressed and valuable experience was gained, a different way of attacking ships developed. Known as dive-bombing, it required a special sort of aircraft and was favoured by both the Germans and the Japanese. It was always more effective, and the Japanese refined their technique by developing a system whereby if the ship's defences were poor or her gun crews were taken by surprise, the pilots would swoop in at mast height and drop their bombs a few moments before reaching their target. With a degree of skill the bomb would hit the side of the vessel at great speed, causing considerable damage. Without the element of surprise on their side, heavily armed ships could inflict heavy losses amongst the low-flying aircraft. An example of how devastating such an attack can be is highlighted in the chapter dealing with the loss of *HMS Cornwall* and *HMS Dorsetshire*. In retrospect it seems strange that even though Britain was amongst the world's leading air powers, it had never developed a dive-bomber of any importance, although in fairness
· it must be said 16 Blackburn Skuas of Nos. 800 and 803 Squadrons of the Fleet Air Arm were responsible for sinking the German cruiser *Königsberg* by dive-bombing in April 1940. And furthermore, even though dive-bombers were used by the Fleet Air Arm, they were never used by the RAF. The Americans had also considered using dive-bombers, particularly against shipping, and had conducted trials using captured German World War One warships. The results were not clear-cut enough for some critics and America accepted that the capital ship, suitably escorted and defended, could not be threatened by aircraft. A number of US Navy Douglas Dauntless dive-bombers were used in the Battle of the Coral Seas and at Midway in May and June 1942 but suffered great losses.

In spite of comparatively poor results by both Allied and Axis flyers in Europe compared with the Japanese in the Pacific, the enormous potential of aircraft against warships had been irrefutably proven which was what the Japanese had always intended. It led to the downfall of the heavy battleship as the backbone of any navy and replaced by aircraft carriers which in future engagements played a dominant role. The absence of all the American aircraft carriers at Pearl Harbour at the time of the Japanese attack was a major blessing as the full weight of the attack fell upon the soon-to-be obsolete battleships.

The operations in the Indian Ocean at the beginning of April 1942 were essential to the establishment of a defence perimeter. Following the destruction of the American-British-Dutch-Australian Command forces in the battles around Java in February and March, the Japanese moved into the Indian Ocean to seek out and destroy British naval power there and support the invasion of Burma by her land forces. Japan entered the war primarily to obtain raw materials, especially oil, from European, particularly Dutch, possessions in South East Asia which were weakly defended because of the war in Europe. Their plans involved an attack on Burma partly because of Burma's own natural resources which included oil from fields around Yenangyaung, as well as minerals such as cobalt and large surpluses of rice, but also to protect the flank of their main attack against Malaya and Singapore and provide a buffer zone to protect the territories they intended to occupy. For this, the Japanese Imperial Naval Headquarters planned to send Vice-Admiral Nagumo's First Carrier Fleet to strike against Ceylon, the heart of British naval power in the East. The colony's main defences seemed woefully inadequate against such a foe, consisting of the Ceylon Defence Force and the Ceylon Navy Volunteer Reserve, both of which were immediately mobilized. Fixed land defences consisted of four coastal batteries at Colombo and five at Trincomalee which had been established shortly before the war began. Added to this, the Royal Navy had naval installations in Trincomalee, whilst the Royal Air Force had established an aerodrome at China Bay long before the war. With Japan's entry into the war, especially after the fall of Singapore, Ceylon became a front-line British base and the Royal Navy's East Indies Station was moved firstly to Colombo and then to Trincomalee.

By making Pearl Harbour-style raids on Colombo and Trincomalee, the Japanese thought they could drive the British Eastern Fleet out of the Indian Ocean, thus protecting their defence perimeter that stretched from Burma to Singapore, against British naval interference. In essence the Japanese strike was actually a four-prong attack with Vice-Admiral Nagumo's larger Second Southern Expeditionary Fleet deployed to the south, initially guided by intelligence from the submarine I7 of the Second Submarine Squadron and backed by aerial reconnaissance. Vice-Admiral Jisaburo Ozawa left Mergui in Burma with a squadron of aircraft which he divided into three parts whilst Rear-Admiral Kurita took the cruisers *Kumano, Suzuya,* and the destroyer *Shirakumo* to sweep north in the upper reaches of the Bay of Bengal. While Ozawa took the carrier *Ryujo* and the cruisers *Chokia, Yura, Assagiri* and *Yugiri* to sweep the centre, Captain Sakiyama took the remaining group of the cruisers *Mikuma* and *Mogami* and the destroyer *Amagiri.* Apart from the obvious practical objective of interfering with sea-borne commerce from the east coast of India, there was also a significant psychological effect. At the time, all of our military strength was committed to saving Burma and there might well have been general panic if India was threatened.

The Admiralty was aware of the dangers to its Eastern Fleet as the collapse of Burma continued. It was mindful of the fact that Nagumo might make another carrier-based raid but despite this, we were so hard-pressed on so many different fronts we did not have enough ships to successfully defend any of them. But we had to hold on to Ceylon because without it, essential convoys from India to Europe and the Western Desert would be in constant danger.

CHAPTER 2

The Allied Response

By April 1942 Japanese forces were close to victory against the Americans in the Philippines whilst at the same time they were steadily advancing into New Guinea and Burma where Rangoon soon fell. It was obvious to all that the British and Indian troops in Burma, as well as the Chinese forces under the American General Joseph Warren Stilwell, could no longer contain the Japanese advance, or even delay it. The Allied priority now was to evacuate as many of the troops as they could. Such a task could be likened to the evacuation of Dunkirk in northern France, except this time the distances were far greater and any offers of outside assistance would be nil. With a road network being almost non-existent and valley escape routes running mostly north and north-east, the retreating troops had no alternative but to walk cross-country towards India. The Japanese First Air Strike Fleet had meanwhile destroyed the remaining Far East Allied naval presence in the Java Sea, attacked Darwin, and was now poised to enter the Indian Ocean unopposed.

There seemed to be a real possibility that within six months of Japan entering the war, the Axis powers would control the Middle and Near East, the Caucasus, India and South East Asia, along with all the vast amount of raw materials they needed for an escalating war effort. The outlook for the Allies was not good, and the British planners focused their attention on the defence of Ceylon, which was seen as the strategic centre of operations now that Singapore had been captured.

The Gun Wharf at Trincomalee.

The port at Trincomalee was about to once again assume its historically strategic importance. Because Ceylon was such an indispensable strategic bastion for the Royal Navy, it was similarly an irresistible military target for the Japanese so the British Chiefs of Staff began to assemble forces to defend the island. With perceived forthcoming attacks on Colombo and Trincomalee, Admiral Somerville's intelligence officers also made plans for a third naval base at Addu Atoll, some 600 miles southwest of Ceylon. It was the southernmost part of the Maldives and was ideal for pre-battle manoeuvres. The Addu Atoll base was designed to be an anchorage and fuelling base but it lacked anti-submarine and anti-aircraft defences. The base, code named Port T, was kept a closely guarded secret for most of the remainder of World War II and the Japanese were not aware of its existence during the April 1942 carrier raids in the Indian Ocean. In fact they did not discover its existence until the later part of the war when they were all but defeated, thus the Royal Navy used it extensively.

Economically, Japan had much to gain from further conquest in Southern Asia and was advancing quickly throughout Burma. She still had to consolidate her hold over Malaya and the East Indies however, and unbeknown to the British, had no immediate plans to invade Ceylon. Above all, to exploit the rich resources of Southern Asia, she needed to secure her sea lines of communication and that required the complete domination of the Pacific. Vice-Admiral Nagumo's fleet with its powerful complement of carriers was not ordered into the Indian Ocean to invade Ceylon, but to eliminate the threat posed by the Royal Navy there so that Japan's full naval force could be directed against the American navy in the South Pacific. Ironically, the formation of the Eastern Fleet invited the very attack it was intended to deter. Buoyant with their success at Pearl Harbour, the Japanese achieved extraordinary success in seizing Malaya and the Dutch East Indies (Indonesia) and with Japanese forces seeming unstoppable, the Indian Ocean lay open and undefended.

Being unaware of the overall Japanese plan, it was generally felt by the Allies that Ceylon would be next to fall, providing an obvious springboard into India. Knowing if this was allowed to happen it would make our convoy routes to the Middle East unsafe so the island had to be protected at all costs. Ceylon could not be allowed to fall to the Japanese but the question was how soon Japan would take action. It was a race against time to increase the island's defences before Japan was ready to strike. The danger was all too real; no one in history had ever conquered so much territory in such a short space of time and the Allied naval strength in the Far East was at a critically low level. It was Churchill's nightmare of the "Most Dangerous and Distressing Moment of the War". The one thing that gave Churchill hope and optimism was America had entered the war on our side. But even so, Churchill was forever mindful of the fact that had Ceylon fallen to the Japanese, it would have brought down the war-time coalition government and compelled Britain to concede defeat.

Confirming this threat in February 1942, Admiral Raeder, the German naval Commander-in-Chief, reported to Hitler that Japan planned to protect her front in the Indian Ocean by capturing the key position of Ceylon, and that she also planned to gain control of the sea in that area by means of superior naval forces. He reported that fifteen Japanese submarines were operating in the Bay of Bengal off Ceylon and also in the straits on both sides of Sumatra and Java. He added that once Japanese battleships, aircraft carriers, submarines, and the Japanese Naval Air Force were based on Ceylon, Britain would be forced to resort to heavily escorted convoys if she wanted to maintain communications with India and the Near East.

Japan was confident that the Americans could be easily eliminated as a force with which to be reckoned but to their credit it was with great heroism and fortitude the Americans held out in the Philippines until mid-May. The Australians meanwhile stoutly defended New Guinea, all of which delayed Japanese plans and gave the Allies valuable breathing space in which to formulate a defensive strategy. Despite this, Japan was still confident at this stage that America could be eliminated as a force that counted in the Western Pacific. Furthermore, she was equally confident that her Ally, Germany would succeed in the Middle East and in Russia, and would cut Britain off from American help. Japan's military and naval forces pressed forward on every front.

Plans to strike westwards into the Indian Ocean and take Ceylon had been prepared by the staff of the Japanese Combined Fleet. Once their battleships, aircraft carriers and submarines were based in Ceylon, their domination over the Indian Ocean would be consolidated. They even considered taking Madagascar, then under Vichy French control. Since the attack on Pearl Harbour there had been many meetings between Vice-Admiral Nomura, the Japanese Naval Attaché in Berlin and Admiral Fricke, Raeder's Chief of Staff, who did much to try to persuade the Japanese to initiate operations that would assist and support Germany's own efforts against Britain. The area in which such co-operation would be most effective was the western Indian Ocean in the direction of the Red Sea and the Persian Gulf. The seizure of Ceylon and Madagascar would be an obvious starting point. This plan, officially known as Operation C, was described as a naval sortie by the fast carrier strike force of the Imperial Japanese Navy, to be conducted from 31st March–10th April 1942 against Allied shipping and bases in the Indian Ocean; it was to be an early engagement in the Pacific campaign. The Japanese fleet would be under the command of

Admiral Nagumo.

Vice-Admiral Chuichi Nagumo who would compel the Allied forces to retreat to East Africa, leaving the Japanese unopposed in the Indian Ocean. On paper it seemed simple enough.

Nagumo was appointed Commander-in-Chief of the First Air Fleet, the Imperial Japanese Navy's main aircraft carrier force, on 10th April 1941, largely due to his seniority as was the Japanese custom, but many contemporaries and historians have doubted his suitability for this command, given his lack of familiarity with naval aviation. He was not in the best of health, having visibly aged both physically and mentally. Physically he suffered from arthritis and mentally he had become a cautious officer who worked hard, meticulously studying all the details of the tactical plans of every operation he was involved in. Admiral Nishizo Tsukahara had some doubts about his appointment and commented, "Nagumo is an officer of the old school, a specialist of torpedo and surface manoeuvres.... He does not have any idea of the capability and potential of naval aviation." However, despite this lack of experience, Nagumo was a strong advocate of combining sea and air power.

Nagumo's flagship, the *Akagi* was designed as a battle cruiser but was converted to an aircraft carrier under the 1922 Washington Naval Treaty at a cost of 53 million Yen (USD\$36 million). She was a unique-looking aircraft carrier. At the time of her construction there were few aircraft carriers in all the navies around the world so there was

The *Akagi*.

no standard design, which resulted in her unique configuration of a triple-flight deck, unconventional port-side island and six 8-inch guns. Already the most expensive ship in the Japanese fleet, she underwent an expensive refit in 1935, giving her the full-length flight deck that she later needed for the Pacific War. The American pilots identified her as a carrier with a boxy superstructure and an improbably high flight deck that towered six-stories above the main deck. After her 1935 refit, the *Akagi* became the first Japanese carrier with a modern large flight deck, but it was the operational experiences aboard her that forged the Japanese naval airpower doctrine. She participated in every major action in the early part of the war, including Pearl Harbour, the attack against Port Darwin, operations in the Indian Ocean, and the Battle of Midway. Unfortunately, with her unique design came an inherent weakness which presented itself during the Battle of Midway. Apart from her anti-aircraft weaponry being of an older and slow-firing design, they were positioned poorly on the port and starboard sides of the ship, twenty or so feet below the flight deck, so the guns on each side could only fire at targets on the same side of the ship. Furthermore, the port side guns were blocked by the island, further reducing the effectiveness of the weapons. This was one of the many reasons why she was fatally attacked at Midway on 4th June 1942 by American dive bombers.

At the beginning of March 1942, Admiral Sir James Somerville was appointed at Churchill's insistence, as Commander-in-Chief of the new British Eastern Fleet, taking command on 26th March. He was said to be 'one of Britain's best fighting admirals', a somewhat grandiose title for someone of his rank but as will be seen later, on paper his command did seem rather impressive. Somerville was recalled from retirement, forced upon him by ill health before the war began, because of his unusual talents and professional ability. He arrived in Ceylon on 24th March, just two days before Vice-Admiral Nagumo and the Japanese fleet set sail from Kendari in the Celebes, and immediately organized a conference to warn his captains

Sir James Somerville.

of the impending Japanese attack. The probable force was given as being two or more carriers, two large six-inch cruisers, possibly several eight-inch cruisers and a large number of destroyers. It was further suggested battleships of the Kongo class might also be in close support. Somerville ventured the date of the attack might be around 31st March.

Somerville's warning of an impending attack by the Japanese was not clear in its detail but it was obvious it would be directed against Colombo or Trincomalee, or even both ports simultaneously. Furthermore, Somerville concluded there were three ways in which the attack could be launched – a) a moonlit night attack followed by a moonlit night landing from carriers; b) a moonlit night attack followed by a dawn landing; and c) a straightforward daylight attack. With a full moon forecast for 1st April and sunrise scheduled for 0559 hrs.

Colombo harbour.

Somerville considered the moonlit night attack followed by a dawn landing would be the most probable method with an approach being made from the south-east.

Air Vice-Marshall d'Albiac, Air Commanding Officer of No. 222 Group who was present at the conference suggested that from his experience the attack would be directed towards Ceylon and the Bay of Bengal in a three-pronged thrust. He proved to be right in every detail. Somerville concurred with d'Albiac's suggestion and added that he thought the attacks would be directed at our naval bases at Colombo and Trincomalee with a third being aimed at our shipping in the Bay of Bengal. For once there was to be no element of surprise, although few of Ceylon's civilian population had any idea of what was to come.

Somerville's battle plan was standard naval procedure. By keeping his fleet well beyond the range of Japanese reconnaissance planes by day but close in at night, it meant he could quickly get his own aircraft within striking distance at daybreak. He wanted to manoeuvre

HMS Hermes.

the Japanese fleet into a night action because he knew his battleships would have gunnery superiority over a carrier force that could not launch its aircraft after dark. He was also mindful of the widely held belief that the Japanese disliked night action and would avoid it at all costs, but this was shown not to be so when the Japanese later started attacking American ships amongst the islands of the South Pacific. Furthermore, Somerville would be fighting relatively close to his bases and sources of supply, whereas Nagumo was far away from his. Any damage to Nagumo's ships by our submarines, destroyers or aircraft would have serious consequences for him. And so, on the evening of 31st March Somerville concentrated his fleet in a position from which he could launch an air attack on the Japanese ships during the night but a cat-and-mouse game of fruitless searching ensued for three days between the two fleets.

When Somerville was appointed, his new Eastern Fleet consisted of the battleship *HMS Warspite*, newly arrived from Freemantle, Australia on which he hoisted his flag as Commander-in-Chief, Eastern Fleet, the aircraft carrier *HMS Hermes*, the destroyer *HMS Vampire* and the cruisers *HMS Emerald* and the *Heemskerck* of the Royal Netherlands Navy. Although under the jurisdiction of the Royal Netherlands Navy, the *Heemskerck*, the destroyer *Isaac Sweers* and eight submarines were all under the direct command of Admiral Somerville. All of these vessels were based at Trincomalee. At Colombo there was the aircraft carrier *HMS Formidable* in which Somerville had taken passage from the UK, together with the cruisers *HMS Cornwall*, *HMS Dorsetshire* which was undergoing a refit, *HMS Enterprise, HMS Dragon, HMS Caledon,* and six destroyers. The battleships *HMS Resolution, HMS Ramillies, HMS Royal Sovereign, HMS Revenge,* the carrier *HMS Indomitable* and eight destroyers that had arrived at Addu Atoll in the Maldives in the previous week were all placed under the command of Vice-Admiral A.U. Willis, Second-in-Command of the Eastern Fleet. Not since the beginning of the war had a squadron of four British battleships made their almost stately way in line ahead like those of Vice-Admiral Willis. And nor had two modern aircraft carriers been available to operate together. *HMS Formidable* had recently returned to service following a refit in the USA where she had taken a number of American-built Martlet fighter aircraft on board in addition to her complement of Albacore biplanes which were essentially a later version of the Swordfish, having much the same performance but now having an enclosed cockpit.

On paper the strength of this new fleet appears to be substantial but in reality Somerville was in an unenviable position. His air cover was far too weak to enable him to seriously oppose the main Japanese carrier force. Unlike the Japanese, the aircraft stationed on our carriers were for the most part obsolescent. Our Albacore torpedo and reconnaissance aircraft were not a great deal better in terms of performance than the Swordfish biplanes with which the Fleet Air Arm had begun the war. When confronting a modern fighter defence force of aircraft like the Zero, day-time attacks by the British would have been both ineffective and suicidal. Somerville had a few Grumman Wildcat and Hurricane fighters in his complement of aircraft but the majority of our fighter aircraft were the two-seater Fulmars which were totally outclassed by the Zeros.

Writing about Admiral Somerville in his book *Fighting Admiral,* Captain Donald MacIntyre pointed out that many of the ships under Somerville's command were old and not in a first-class condition. Except for the R class battleships, there were hardly two ships of the same class so grouping them into squadrons was a puzzle made more difficult by the fact that there was not a list of the individual captains

HMS Indomitable with her Albacore aircraft ready for take-off.

or their seniorities aboard the flagship. This fleet was totally under-strength and insufficient for the enormous task of guarding the whole Indian Ocean from the western approaches to Australia, to the Cape of Good Hope and the convoy routes to the Suez Canal. Furthermore, his bases were ill-equipped to supply his needs. There were clearly real grounds for anxiety over the outcome of an incursion into the Indian Ocean by the well-trained and highly disciplined Japanese carrier force under Vice-Admiral Nagumo.

Conversely, if Somerville could get his Strike Force close enough to Nagumo's heavy ships at night, he knew he had a good chance of inflicting severe damage and redressing the balance in our favour. In subsequent discussions Somerville had with Captain Agar of the *Dorsetshire* he told him this was very much to the fore in his mind. Agar pointed out that with the *Emerald* and *Enterprise* alone, given their speed and offensive armament, Somerville's plan was workable.

Agar considered that against this reasoning there was the solid background of our critical position in the Indian Ocean, and the vital necessity of maintaining our convoys to India via Bombay and the Middle East via Aden. A defeat would uncover these routes and lay open the way, not only for an invasion of India, where there were hardly any defences, but also cut us off from the Middle East until the position could be restored. The risk therefore, of seeking a confrontation was one that should not be considered. This was endorsed in a personal message to Somerville from the First Sea Lord in which he strongly advised him not to allow his fleet to become engaged with anything except inferior forces until the Eastern Fleet could be reinforced. The First Sea Lord often sent such messages to the Flag Officers when conducting operations, obviously intended to influence their judgement and decisions. Somerville had no choice but to adopt a purely defensive strategy with his fleet guarding these routes, with Colombo as his base, hoping that at some point he might be able to lure Nagumo further west, when he would have an opportunity of striking at him with his light forces.

In his book *Destroyer Man*, Rear Admiral A.F. Pugsley, at the time Captain of *HMS Paladin*, a destroyer that later rescued the survivors of the *Dorsetshire*, described the Eastern Fleet as being 'reminiscent of naval formations he hadn't seen since his days as a midshipman in 1918; it steamed along "in line ahead"'. The battleships were in fact, all veterans of the First World War with a squadron speed of only 18 knots. Pugsley confirmed it was indeed the largest fleet to have been assembled in the war and overall looked impressive, but he was quick to point out its weaknesses. Apart from the veteran battleships, the six-inch cruisers with their ancient guns were of limited range and the eight-inch cruisers with their lack of armour plating and meagre anti-aircraft armament were no match for their opposite numbers in the Japanese navy. From the bridge of his own ship, *Paladin*, Pugsley could only look down in frustration at his four-inch guns projecting from shields designed for 4.7-inch guns. Other destroyers in the fleet were similarly poorly equipped. Furthermore, the aircraft carrier *Hermes*, the only carrier to be designed and built as such, had only a few aircraft aboard and was capable of only a moderate speed, whilst many of the other ships had no experience in operating as part of a fleet, having been deployed on independent duties, like ferrying aircraft, since being first commissioned.

In contrast to the British fleet, the Japanese fleet consisted mostly of modern, fast ships manned by well-trained crews; its aircraft carriers each had large numbers of aircraft flown by highly expert and seasoned pilots. But unlike the British carriers, the Japanese carriers were not armour plated above the water line so they were capable of carrying more aircraft for a similar displacement. Between Nagumo's five carriers, he had 318 aircraft compared with our 90 in the three carriers of the Eastern Fleet. His battleships, even though as old as ours, were much modernized and were considerably faster. But their role was a minor one; the Japanese emphasis was on its aircraft carriers. In a conventional sea battle, opposition to the Japanese fleet would have been nothing short of suicidal.

We were in a situation not too dissimilar to that which had in previous wars been forced upon our enemies, ie the weaker fleet was only of value so long as it was kept away from a direct encounter with the enemy, yet tying down the enemy fleet and preventing it from taking advantage of its command of the sea. It was a policy known as The Fleet in Being.

Somerville divided his fleet into two parts, Force A, a fast division consisting of *Warspite, Indomitable, Formidable, Cornwall, Dorsetshire, Emerald, Enterprise,* and six destroyers all operating under his immediate orders, and Force B, the remainder of the fleet under the command of Vice-Admiral Willis, which would be kept within supporting distance to the west of him. Catalina flying boat patrols were arranged to cover a distance of 420 miles from Colombo between the bearings of 110 degrees to 154 degrees to try to locate the Japanese fleet. It was appreciated that the Japanese might approach from any direction but as there were only six Catalinas available (plus one in reserve), not more than three could be on patrol at any one time.

Somerville had no illusions about Force B whose ships were old, slow and capable of only short-range patrols. The cruisers and the destroyers had never practiced manoeuvres together and were all badly in need of repairs and refits. He knew they would be of little use against a carrier-led attack so his best course of action would be to keep them in reserve for other tasks, such as acting as cover for convoys in the Indian Ocean. Force A would therefore take the brunt of repulsing the anticipated raids.

And so on 30th March Somerville's Force A set sail for the rendezvous point with Vice-Admiral Willis' Force B. The following day Japanese submarine patrols were spotted 360 miles from Colombo. Somerville concluded these were intended for the dual purpose of providing reconnaissance and serving as a screen through which the Japanese ships could withdraw after their attack on Ceylon. An Albacore aircraft from the *Formidable* flew ashore to request the Deputy C-in-C to arrange a patrol in the area where the submarines had been spotted, in addition to the regular Catalina patrols.

Two considerations governed the fleet's movements during the night of 31st March/1st April – a) the necessity of avoiding the enemy's daylight search area until after dark, ie sunset was at 1809 hrs on that day, in order to achieve the element of surprise; and b) to be at a convenient distance from the enemy's probable position for flying off its aircraft for the attack. This put the fleet some 120 miles from the Japanese at 1800 hrs on 31st March.

Meanwhile Vice-Admiral Willis aboard his flagship *Resolution* had sailed from Addu Atoll on 29th March with the Third Battle Squadron, Force B, of *Indomitable* and nine destroyers, making the rendezvous point during the afternoon of 31st March. The disposition of the two Forces was now in place. Somerville tried for three days and two nights to hold his chosen defence and attack positions south of Ceylon but by the evening of 2nd April he concluded that either the information about the date of the strike had been wrong, or the Japanese were playing a waiting game, trying to catch the British fleet in the harbour at night.

Force A steered a course to the north until dark, then turned eighty degrees at a speed of 15 knots. They maintained a continuous AVS search ahead and to the south throughout the night. The Japanese estimated flying-off point was reached at 0230 hrs on 1st April but nothing was sighted and the course was altered to the southwest to withdraw outside the enemy's search area. Force B meanwhile kept some 20 miles to the west, rejoining Somerville as ordered at 0800 hrs on April 1st. Throughout that day the fleet cruised south of Ceylon and during the afternoon, *Dorsetshire* joined Force A, having abruptly stopped her refit in order to take part in the operation.

With the fleet having been at sea for three days and two nights, the probability of it being located by Japanese submarines was increasing. No further information had been received of the likelihood of an air attack on Ceylon and it was thought either the Japanese timing might have been upset, or they might have become aware of our fleet's concentration and were waiting till it had returned to harbour for fuel and supplies. Alternatively, it was always a possibility that the British deductions might well have been wrong from the start, but that seemed highly unlikely.

On the strength of these considerations, Admiral Somerville decided to carry out a smaller sweep to the east than had been conducted on the two previous nights and if nothing was sighted, to abandon the operation. Again it proved fruitless and at 2100 hrs on April 2nd he made a costly error by setting course for Addu Atoll to refuel. At 0520 hrs the following morning *Fortune* was sent to the assistance of SS *Glen Shiel* who had been torpedoed. *Dorsetshire* and *Cornwall* were dispatched to Colombo, the former to continue with her interrupted refit and the latter for convoy escort duties. *Hermes* and *Vampire* were sent to Trincomalee to prepare for a special operation, Operation Ironclad, the occupation of Diego Suarez in Madagascar.

A crucial part of Britain's plan to protect the Indian Ocean was to establish a military presence on Madagascar, centred at Diego Suarez. Madagascar was a French colony under the control of the Vichy government and although many Free French were now fighting alongside the British, the French Vichy government was a very different proposition; it sided with Germany. It was feared that the Vichy government might cede the whole of Madagascar to Japan, or alternatively permit the Japanese navy to establish bases on the island.

As early as November 1941 the Vichy government had submitted to German pressure and agreed to Japanese occupation of the island if it became necessary.

The Allies' fears of Japan establishing bases in Madagascar stemmed from the Vichy government, in siding with the Axis Powers, had allowed the Japanese into French Indo-China to use its bases, which gave them access to Malaya and Singapore. History looked like repeating itself and it was feared the Japanese would now move into the huge natural deep water port of Diego Suarez on the northern tip of Madagascar which would give them a dominant position in the Indian Ocean and threaten the convoy route running up East Africa to Egypt. Japanese submarines could be based there and they had the longest range of any at the time, more than 10,000 miles (16,000 km) in some cases. They were also impressive in their size. Whereas the largest German U-boat at that time was some 1,600 tons, the Japanese subs were typically 2,000 tons. Their size made them difficult to manoeuvre but to compensate for this they had a high surface speed and a long range. Furthermore, they were designed to carry a midget submarine or a small reconnaissance float-plane. What a bonus! It is believed these midget submarines were used with great effect at Pearl Harbour. Were these vessels allowed to use bases on Madagascar, Allied lines of communications would be greatly affected across a region stretching from the Pacific and Australia, to the Middle East and as far as the South Atlantic. The British had to occupy the island as a precautionary measure and secure the African coast.

A pre-emptive invasion of Madagascar was therefore launched by the British on 5th May 1942, called Operation Ironclad in which troops landed on the north-western tip of the island in an attempt to capture the port from the rear. The surprise landings themselves were successful but as the force moved inland they encountered determined resistance. The French had built a defensive line to protect their rear and it was well defended. A frontal assault the next morning against the French position defending Antsirane finally succeeded and additional shelling by British warships forced the local Vichy commander to surrender.

The French defenders capitulated on 7th May, but the Vichy governor of the island retreated to the south of the island with his forces and Vichy resistance continued until November 1942.

It was later learned that despite our assuming Madagascar to be a prime Japanese military target, it was not so. Japan was more intent on placating Germany than extending her influence so far westwards and the operation fell considerably short of what had been expected by the Germans.

Meanwhile Admiral Somerville was convinced by this time either something had happened to delay the Japanese attack on Ceylon or that their objective had been misunderstood. But Vice-Admiral Nagumo was not playing a waiting game; he was actually making his approach as planned to the south of Ceylon on a westerly course. He was lacking any information from his submarine patrols as to the whereabouts of the British fleet and had mistakenly assumed it must have put into port at Colombo where he hoped to smash it the next morning in another Pearl Harbour style of attack. For their part, Somerville's staff had simply assessed the date of the raid several days too early. The Japanese fleet was on its way. Vice-Admiral Nagumo would be operating at an extended range and was refuelling his ships at sea before pressing on westwards.

In the late afternoon of 4th April the Japanese fleet was spotted some 360 miles south of Dondra Head, the southernmost tip of Ceylon. It was anticipated the expected attack would come the following morning, 5th April. Admiral Somerville was 600 miles away at Addu Atoll and was in no position to do anything. Measures were taken immediately to correct the British mistakes. Admiral Sir Geoffrey Layton, C-in-C, Ceylon, whose wide-ranging powers subordinated the civilian authorities, ordered all defences at Colombo to be at general quarters by 3am on 5th April and with most of the ships already at sea, the rest were ordered to raise steam and set sail in all haste.

CHAPTER 3

Political Divisions as Ceylon Prepares

So far the war had not affected Ceylon or its people directly, even though many of the young Europeans living on the island had "gone off to war". Their women and children had also departed, at the authorities' suggestion, to South Africa. But as the build-up of numbers of aircraft, ships and manpower began, those left in Ceylon slowly began to realize something big was about to happen. But it was not only the war that concerned many at this time. There were also long-standing political issues to be addressed, chiefly over demands for Home Rule and Independence, which had received little publicity, and as this is a side issue, albeit an important one, in the story, now seems a pertinent time to outline some of the major arguments.

As Admiral Sir Geoffrey Layton began implementing his defence strategy for the imminent Japanese assault, the Ceylonese people prepared to put their differences with Britain to one side until the cessation of hostilities with Japan. Across the Palk Strait in India the attitude of its National Congress was the complete opposite and at times it seemed like India was using the war to drive home its demands for independence. The political situation in India was intrinsically entwined with that of Ceylon. Both were British Crown Colonies, part of the influential British Empire, and whereas, as we now know, it was not Japan's intention to occupy Ceylon, it was an important stepping stone into India and Burma. Throughout both colonies there was a strong anti-British feeling which escalated within some sections of the indigenous population as their hopes ran high for liberation by the Japanese. However, as Japanese troops approached the borders of India, pressure mounted from China, the United States and Britain to resolve the issue of the future status of India before the end of the war.

The British had ruled India since the mid-nineteenth century, which the Indians were understandably unhappy about and the Indian National Congress actively promoted a policy of non-violent resistance to British rule. On 23rd March 1942 the recently appointed Lord Privy Seal, Sir Stafford Cripps, came to New Delhi to discuss the British Government's Draft Declaration which offered India Dominion status after the war but otherwise conceded few changes to the Government of India Act of 1935. It was unacceptable to the Congress Working Committee who rejected it outright. The Indians had been demanding a greater role in governing their country since the late-nineteenth century. Their contribution to the British war effort during the First World War was such that even the more conservative elements in the British political establishment felt there was a need for constitutional change and it resulted in the Government of India Act, 1919. That Act introduced a system of government known as provincial diarchy, which was essentially a division of the executive branch of each provincial government into authoritarian and popularly responsible sections. The first was composed of executive councillors, appointed, as before, by the Crown, whilst the second was composed of ministers who were chosen by the governor from the elected members of the provincial legislature. These latter ministers were Indians.

The various fields, or subjects of administration, were divided between the councillors and the ministers, being named reserved and transferred subjects respectively. The reserved subjects came under the heading of law and order, and included justice, the police, land revenue, and irrigation. The transferred subjects (i.e., those under the control of Indian ministers) included local self-government, education, public health, public works, and agriculture, forests and fisheries. The purse strings would however, still be in the hands of the British. The system ended with the introduction of provincial autonomy in 1935.

The intention had originally been for a review of India's constitutional arrangements and those princely states that were willing to accede to it. However, division between Congress and Muslim representatives proved to be a major factor in preventing agreement about much of the important detail of how federation would work in practice, so against this background the new Conservative government in London decided to go ahead with drafting its own proposals. A White Paper was drawn up and on the basis of this the Government of India Bill was framed. It was not only extremely detailed in its content but it was riddled with 'safeguards' designed to enable the British Government to intervene whenever it saw the need in order to maintain British responsibilities and interests. These safeguards were strengthened, and indirect elections were reinstated for the Central Legislative Assembly. The Bill became law in August 1935.

As a result of this, although the Government of India Act 1935 was intended to go some way towards meeting Indian demands, both the detail of the Bill and the lack of Indian involvement in drafting its contents meant that the Act met with a lukewarm response at best in India, while still proving too radical for a significant element in Britain. Indian demands were by now centring on British India achieving constitutional parity with the existing Dominions such as Canada and Australia, which would have meant complete autonomy within the British Commonwealth. A significant element in British political circles doubted that the Indians were capable of running their country on this basis, and saw Dominion status as something that might, perhaps, be aimed for after a long period of gradual constitutional development, with sufficient safeguards in place. This tension between and within Indian and British views resulted in the clumsy compromise of the 1935 Act having no preamble of its own, but keeping in place the 1919 Act's preamble even while repealing the remainder of that Act. Unsurprisingly, this was seen in India as yet more mixed messages from the British, suggesting at best a lukewarm attitude and at worst suggesting a minimum necessary approach towards satisfying Indian desires.

In response the Indian government issued a statement based on the original 'Quit India' resolution drafted by Gandhi but rejected by the Congress Working Committee in favour of a modified version submitted by Nehru. It stated that the Committee was of the opinion that Britain was incapable of defending India and that there was eternal conflict between Indian and British interest. It accused the British government of having no trust in India's political parties, and the Indian Army had been maintained for the most part to hold India in subjugation and was completely segregated from the general population who could in no sense regard it as their own.

Japan's quarrel, it was suggested, was not with India. She was said to be warring against the British Empire. And India's participation in the war was not with the consent of the representatives of the Indian people but was purely a British undertaking. If India were freed, her first step would probably be to negotiate peace with Japan. The Congress was of the opinion that if the British withdrew, India would be able to defend herself in the event of the Japanese, or any other aggressor, attacking India. The Committee was firmly of the opinion that the British should withdraw from India and rebuked the British claim that they should remain in India, if for no other reason than for the protection of the Indian princes which they saw as additional proof of British determination to maintain their hold over India because its princes faced no fear or threat from an unarmed India.

Assurance was given to the Japanese Government that India bore no enmity, either towards Japan or any other nation but only sought freedom from all alien domination. Towards this end, the Committee was of the opinion that India, whilst welcoming universal sympathy, did not need foreign military aid. India would attain her freedom through her non-violent strength and would retain it. Therefore, the Committee hoped that Japan would not have any designs on India, but if they did attack India, and Britain made no response to its appeal for help, the Committee would expect all those who look to the Congress for guidance to offer complete non-violent non-co-operation to the Japanese forces, and not to render any assistance to them.

The dilemma was that if India offered the British complete non-co-operation when they were fighting, it would be as good as allowing the country to deliberately fall into Japanese hands, but alternatively the only way of demonstrating non-co-operation with the Japanese was not to put any obstacles in the way of the British forces. It was the classic 'chicken and egg' situation. Whilst the policy of non-co-operation against the Japanese forces would be restricted to a comparatively small number of extremists and had to succeed if it was to be complete and genuine, true self-government (*swaraj*) rested with the millions of ordinary Indian citizens who were wholeheartedly working for a constructive programme of Independence.

The failure of Cripps' mission further estranged the Congress and the British Government. Gandhi seized upon this, the advances of the Japanese in South-East Asia and the general frustration with the British in India, and called for a voluntary British withdrawal from India. It was hardly a propitious moment for Cripps. Nehru and other Indian leaders had just been released from prison where they had been jailed for making inflammatory anti-British speeches. Their release almost coincided with the Japanese attack on Pearl Harbour, happening four days before it. Britain's motives might have been brought into question about this had the release date followed, and not preceded, the attack.

With Britain being so preoccupied with the war in Europe, the Indian leaders saw an opportunity to cut their ties with British rule and pursued it vigorously. They believed they had the support of the USA and Roosevelt had said so. But it was not in the Indians' psyche to do anything other than 'non-co-operation', or passive resistance. Instead, Nehru was faced with the dilemma of choosing between continued dependence on Britain or annexation, and conquest by, or at least subservience to, Japan. India's leaders badly wanted independence and seemed totally oblivious to the events unfolding around them. It was like they had stuck their head in the sand and hoped the problem would go away. Gandhi is said to have told the British, 'Don't leave

India to Japan, but leave India to the Indians in an orderly manner.' It could not be done. With its 390m population consisting mostly of poverty-stricken, tradition-bound, caste-ridden people, disunited by religion, politics, race, language and social distinction it had no chance of self-rule, well not in 1942 at least.

Since as early as 1940, Britain had firmly believed that India's wholehearted support for the war against Japan was essential. It was thought that because Japan was so heavily committed in Indo-China and China she would hesitate at entering the war on a broader basis, if convinced that India was firmly against her. Indians who knew or cared about such things did co-operate with the British but only in return for complete autonomy. Indeed, many serving Indian soldiers would never have wished to serve under a government in which the Indian National Congress formed the predominant element.

To the combatants in World War II India was a sticking point. It could not be abandoned because from a global perspective its importance might become incalculable. If the German offensive against Russia continued unchecked, the Middle East oil supplies, vital to the West, would be in danger. If India allied itself to Japan, or just followed a policy of non-co-operation with her, it could close the gap between Japan and Germany by over 2,000 miles. China would also be cut off from all effective help, and with the German and Italian armies securely entrenched on Egypt's frontier, until El Alamein in November, the Axis threat from that direction, with the prospect to the Allies of losing the Suez Canal, seemed even more pressing than the threat through the Caucasus.

But such a broad strategic view does not take into account the enormous difficulties of communications that would have arisen. For example, between Burma and India there are no major road networks, only dirt tracks. Afghanistan had scarcely any road or rail communications at this time. Only sea and air routes would have been open to Japan which is another reason why it had to gain control of the Indian Ocean.

Across the Palk Strait in Ceylon its government, headed by Sir Don Baron Javatilaka, presented a more reassuring offer than India had and assured the British government of its continued support. Much of the population gave unstinting and ungrudging support to Britain and her Allies. But even though facing an imminent attack and possible invasion, not everyone was so supportive, central to which was a long-standing resistance to the British amongst certain parts of the indigenous population. An underlying mood of an anti-British mind-set prevailed amongst some of the islanders, fuelled by the Japanese successes, notably at Pearl Harbour and Singapore, as well as the sinking of the *Prince of Wales* and the *Repulse*, and the public mood in Ceylon was starting to turn in support of the Japanese. It was encouraged by successful Japanese-trained and directed rebellions in Indonesia, and support for the Japanese forces in Thailand, Sinkiang and the Philippines grew with many of the Ceylonese people hoping that the Japanese would liberate them as well. Two young members of the governing party, Junius Richard Jayawardene, later to become President of Sri Lanka, and Dudley Senanayake, later the country's

HMS Prince of Wales.

HMS Repulse.

third Prime Minister, even held discussions with the Japanese with a view to collaboration and ousting the British from Ceylon but were immediately stopped by the much older and wiser D.S. Senanayake, the first Prime Minister, who went on to lead Ceylon to independence in 1948. Leading this anti-war movement was the Lanka Sama Samaia Party, a Trotskyist political party which supported the independence movement and made it clear that it did not side with either the Axis powers or the Allies, considering the war to be an international one. The Communist Party of Ceylon initially supported the anti-war movement as they saw it as a war of Imperialists, but in 1941 when Germany attacked the Soviet Union they joined the pro-war movement in support of the British, now calling it a People's War. But most of Ceylon's population feared a Japanese victory and supported the allegiance shown by Sir Don Baron Javatilaka.

It was time to review Ceylon's defences, such as they were. Even though the British had occupied the coastal areas of Ceylon since 1796, the colony had not had a regular garrison of British troops since 1917. Instead it relied on the Ceylon Defence Force and the Ceylon Navy

Volunteer Reserve which were now quickly mobilized and increased in strength. As with all other British Colonies conscription was not implemented in Ceylon. The Ceylonese were however, encouraged to volunteer for service and many did so throughout the war, with most joining the Ceylon Defence Force. The fixed land defences established just before the war, consisted of four coastal batteries at Colombo and five at Trincomaleee. Air defences were expanded in 1941 with the RAF occupying the civilian airfield at Ratmalana, near Colombo with its station headquarters set up at Kandawala. Another airbase was rapidly built at Koggala, near Galle and several temporary airstrips were built across the country with the largest at Colombo Racecourse. Several RAF squadrons were then sent to Ceylon as reinforcements and the Allied air cover included 22 Hurricanes, 14 Spitfires and 6 Fulmers. Also a number of Blenheim bombers were based at Trincomalee from where it was hoped they could attack the Japanese carriers. This then was the sum total of Ceylon's defences as a front-line British base against such an imposing enemy who had just caused so much devastation on the American fleet at Pearl Harbour.

Following the fall of Singapore in February, Admiral Sir Geoffrey Layton who had been superseded by but later succeeded, Admiral Sir Tom Phillips as Commander-in-Chief, Far Eastern Fleet, had no headquarters and no fleet to command so he was sent to Ceylon to oversee its defence. Back in London the Chiefs of Staff Committee had decided that in every theatre of war there must be a structure of unified command from which each of the three services should take their orders. It was a policy that was to be followed for the rest of the war on every front and despite initial heated arguments about it, there can be no doubt it made good sense. Layton was appointed Commander-in-Chief, Ceylon with powers that far exceeded those of the civilian Governor, Sir Andrew Caldecott. Using his new powers and with the assistance of Sir Oliver Goonetilleke (who later became Ceylon's first Ceylonese Governor-General) as Civil Defence Commissioner, he organized the island's defence strategy with great speed. Time was of the essence; there was much to be done. Defences and organisation were inadequate; harbour facilities were inefficiently run with many transports left waiting in exposed anchorages; and the island's radar, civil defence and air raid system all needed improving. A new airstrip had to be prepared which unfortunately cut across Colombo's racecourse, and several houses, including that of the Chief Justice of the island, had to be demolished. In Ceylon the monsoon winds blow from the southwest for half of the year and from the northeast for the other half, which necessitated for a single runway instead of the more usual triangular configuration.

Extra troops were drafted to the island, some unintentionally. The Prime Minister of Australia, Mr J.J. Curtin had called for the withdrawal of Australian troops from North Africa when the Japanese began their campaign in Asia as it seemed likely they would be needed for home defence. At first Churchill rebuffed such a move but as an attack on Australia seemed evermore likely, everyone sided with Curtin. The 7th Australian Division embarked for home and despite an attempt to have part of the Division diverted to Rangoon, Curtin stood firm in his demand. The 16th and 17th Brigades were meanwhile encamped at Ceylon near Colombo awaiting transport home, as was the 24th East African Brigade who although bound for Burma, were not due to be there until much later. The 34th Indian Division were also here at this time. As an attack on Ceylon became increasingly likely and all ships dispersed to sea, they all became embroiled in the defence of Ceylon.

But it was in the air that Ceylon needed the most effective reinforcements. Prior to March there had not been any modern aircraft in this particular theatre of war. Old biplanes like Wapitis and Wildebeests were still in service as the demands of the West and the Middle East had made it impossible for them to be replaced. However, that month two squadrons of Hurricanes, Nos.30 and 261 were brought in from North Africa on the carrier *HMS Indomitable*. The two squadrons had initially been intended for Java but Admiral Layton exercised his new authority and applied such pressure that they were diverted to Ceylon. After leaving Singapore and before his arrival in Ceylon, Layton had spent some weeks in Java organizing a naval headquarters there so his opinion that the Hurricanes were of little use in Java and would inevitably be lost in the coming conflict was founded on better intelligence than was available to the Air Ministry.

Seven miles south of Colombo is Ceylon's civilian airport at Ratmalana. Its runway was too short for military aircraft so work began extending it so that its length was almost doubled. The RAF moved in and their Hurricanes of No.30 Squadron, newly arrived from the North African desert campaign, and the Blenheim medium bombers of No.11 Squadron, veterans of Greece, Crete and the Middle East, were based there. Ratmalana lost its civilian status and the RAF commandeered the villa of Colonel Sir John Kotelawala as the station's HQ. The surrounding coconut plantations made excellent camouflage and cooling shade for the airstrip.

To begin with, No.258, a virtually new Squadron re-formed with Hurricanes and new personnel after service in Malaya with Buffaloes, joined their comrades at Ratmalana but later moved to the new racecourse airstrip. Its pilots came from the UK, Australia, New Zealand, Rhodesia, Canada, the USA, South Africa and Argentina; it was truly international. Two Squadrons of Fleet Air Arm Fulmars, Nos.803 and 806 also reached Ratmalana during March, having flown in from Alexandria. Whilst at Alexandria these two squadrons had flown Hurricanes, having had close ties with the RAF's No.30 Squadron with whom they had been designated as No.269 Wing. They were not best-pleased at being re-equipped with slower, far less manoeuvrable two-seater Fulmars after handing over their Hurricanes to other units for continued use in the desert.

Adjoining Trincomalee harbour on the east coast is China Bay airfield which takes its name from a neighbouring sector of the harbour. It abuts on to Malay Cove from where the Catalina flying-boats of the Dutch 321 Squadron operated and in March 1942 it became a hive of activity. The China Bay airfield had been designed and solidly built on RAF peacetime principles, and it was here that No.261 Squadron came from the *Indomitable* in March following their moment of glory in the defence of Malta with their old Gladiator biplanes named Faith,

Hope and Charity. They had by now been re-equipped with Hurricanes. The pilots of No.261 Squadron were not used to taking off from aircraft carriers but they had no choice when they left the *Indomitable* to fly the final fifty miles to Ceylon. One of these pilots, Sgt. Whittaker, developed engine trouble soon after take-off and had to return to the carrier. For him it was an extremely difficult manoeuvre, landing on the short deck, especially as his aircraft was not fitted with arrestor gear. •

One strange-sounding Squadron that was based at China Bay was No.273 whose pilots were a collection of naval and marine flyers, even though it was officially classed as an RAF Squadron, such were the lengths made to muster every available aircraft for the forthcoming battle. It later became a front-line Hurricane Squadron but at the time had Fulmars, an old Seal biplane and three American-built Martlet fighters, but as there was insufficient ·5-inch ammunition for their guns (the RAF used ·303), they had to be hurriedly replaced. A Swordfish Squadron of the Fleet Air Arm, No. 788, was formed from spare aircraft and reinforcements from England and they too were based at China Bay. Despite being an old and slow biplane, this particular aircraft was still very much in use as a front-line torpedo-bomber by the Fleet Air Arm even though it was greatly outmoded in performance and vulnerability, but it has to be remembered how effective the Fleet Air Arm's Swordfish aircraft had been against the Italian Fleet at Taranto in November 1940.

At Koggala, a land-locked lagoon south of the old Dutch fort of Galle on Ceylon's southwest coast was a small force of Catalina long-range flying boats, which completed the complement of No.222 Group, RAF and the Ceylon contingent of Naval Air Stations, Eastern Theatre. The Catalina was American-built and because it was designed for long-range patrols, it was roomy inside with many creature comforts like an electric stove and bunk beds. Such was its suitability for the role it had to undertake, it was never superseded throughout the war years. Unlike the Hurricane and the Spitfire, the Catalina was never a glamorous aircraft but it was a highly dependable work-horse which earned it much respect from those who flew them.

From a naval perspective Ceylon had two useable harbours. On the east coast is the large natural harbour of Trincomalee, entered through a narrow channel from Koddiar Bay, itself well-protected from the open sea and easily capable of taking the largest of fleets in its safe anchorage. It is said to be the finest natural harbour in the world. The Royal Navy's East Indies Station was based at Trincomalee, having moved there from Colombo where it had initially been based. Of the few ships anchored at Trincomalee, all were naval vessels, except for one merchantman, the *Sagaing*, which was anchored in the centre of the harbour and for some unknown reason was not moved. Perhaps it was because she felt safe with a squadron of Hurricanes based only half-a-mile away at China Bay. At this time Trincomalee harbour was only half-finished, and even though a much better target than Colombo, it was felt both would almost certainly be subjected to early enemy attack.

On the west coast was Colombo harbour, which was comparatively small and generally crowded with merchant ships. It was essentially a

Colombo harbour.

commercial port used largely by the convoys but at this time it was fast becoming something of a shipping refugee centre with many vessels having come from Singapore. It was full to overflowing with ships of all sizes from large liners used as troop transports to small Dutch coasters which had escaped from the Java Seas, offering a tempting target to the Japanese.

Unbeknown to the Japanese, an emergency naval base had been established at Addu Atoll, a remote coral island at the southernmost point of the Maldives, some 600-miles southwest of Ceylon. Prior to the start of the war the Admiralty had had the remarkable foresight to organize and prepare, in the greatest secrecy, an emergency base where the fleet could anchor, take on oil, stores and ammunition, and be free from the fear of attack by submarines. Even though it was perfectly adequate, this anchorage was far from ideal, being little more than a large lagoon offering little shelter from the sea, and it lacked both anti-submarine and anti-aircraft defences. There were adequate supplies there but its greatest asset was that its presence was largely unknown to the Japanese. Addu Atoll was in a truly splendid strategical position from which an inferior force could operate against Nagumo's aircraft carriers and heavy ships should they enter the Indian Ocean. Admiral Somerville decided therefore to base the fleet temporarily at Addu Atoll from where he could operate in reasonable security. By the time the Eastern Fleet was formed, this base was well established, complete with a seaplane unit for local reconnaissance, and upon its arrival at Addu Atoll it was greeted by Captain Charles Hammill and his Mobile Naval Defence Base team.

And so the scene was set for the anticipated Japanese onslaught. Valuable lessons had been learned following the attack on Pearl Harbour and the later Japanese attack on Port Darwin, Northern Australia in February 1942 when twelve ships were sunk. There were too many ports and harbours where anti-aircraft defences were limited and where air protection was incapable of defeating an enemy attack in any strength, so the Admiralty ordered that if any threat of a carrier-borne attack developed in the Indian Ocean, the principal ports of Calcutta, Madras,

Trincomalee and Colombo were to be cleared of all shipping in good time. In each of these ports there were always valuable targets and in Calcutta alone there was usually on average 250,000 tons of merchant shipping at any one time. Everyone now expected the Japanese to take full advantage of the naval supremacy they had so swiftly won in the Indian Ocean.

As soon as it was learned that an attack on Ceylon was imminent, Vice-Admiral Sir Geoffrey Arbuthnot, C-in-C East Indies Station, issued the order that the ports and harbours in Ceylon, as well as those in India, were to be cleared. All ships capable of raising steam were ordered to put to sea as quickly as possible, but there were a few who could not and had to remain at anchor. Forty-eight ships weighed anchor on the evening of 4th April and scattered to the west and northwest coast, lying at intervals of a few miles and looking as one pilot commented, "like beads on a necklace". A similar order was given in Calcutta where over seventy ships put to sea. The preparations had been made; Ceylon now awaited the imminently expected attack.

At this time no one knew that Vice-Admiral Nagumo's force had actually set sail from Kendari in Indonesia, and not Singapore as expected, on 26th March. Kendari was an important objective of the Japanese because of its airfield, which could be used to over-rule the sea lanes between Australia and the Dutch East Indies, and to bomb Dutch bases on Java and other islands. The garrison at Kendari had been surprised by a Japanese landing on the night of 23–24th January 1942 and put up little resistance before Kendari and the intact airfield were captured. Furthermore, Kendari was several days sailing time nearer to Ceylon than Singapore and Nagumo's fleet entered the Indian Ocean through the Ombai Straits unopposed. Everyone expected the Japanese to strike on 31st March.

Somerville transferred his flag to the *Warspite* and since the enemy did not appear, made ready on 1st and 2nd April for joint manoeuvres. Unfortunately some of the smaller ships and the R-class battleships, which had not been designed for long-range work in the tropics, had to return to port for more fuel and fresh water. By the evening of 2nd

HMS Warspite.

April it was felt that the whole thing might have been a false alarm. But no, Nagumo had the enormous advantage that his Force could be kept together as a whole and he could choose where and when to strike. His position could not have been more different to that of Somerville who following the earlier Battle of the Java Seas, accepted he had the only ships available in the Indian Ocean for the protection of the all-important route to the Middle East from the Cape of Good Hope up the East African coast along which, in the reverse direction, essential oil supplies were brought. Knowing how powerful the Japanese fleet was, Somerville knew he could not risk loosing any of his ships. His safest tactic would be to hold his battleships back but at the ready if needed, and follow the enemy's movements by aerial reconnaissance. The one flaw with this plan was that the Swordfish and Albacore aircraft used for this purpose had a range of less than 200 miles so the intelligence Somerville would need would have to be supplied by a longer-range Catalina and at that time there was only one serviceable Catalina available.

HMS Dorsetshire had been undergoing a refit when the fleet was ordered out to sea and with the Japanese threat not seeming to be imminent, she was ordered back to Colombo to continue with the work. Her sister ship, *HMS Cornwall* accompanied her as she was due to escort convoy SU4 to Australia after it had picked up more troops at Colombo. *Hermes* needed her boilers cleaning and was dispatched to Trincomalee with the destroyer *Vampire.* The remainder of the fleet returned to Addu Atoll for refuelling and the general mood was slightly relaxed. A careful eye was kept to the east however, and Swordfish aircraft maintained their patrols. Destroyers patrolled the area forward of the main fleet, but where was Vice-Admiral Nagumo? It was most perplexing.

Nagumo was in fact rounding the southern tip of Sumatra. He planned, as he had done at Pearl Harbour a few months before, to launch his air attack on Colombo on a Sunday, in this case 5th April. Had Somerville been able to wait in his chosen position, south of Ceylon, the two forces would have inevitably met in a battle which would have been the biggest conflict of the war, probably resulting in a total disaster for the ill-trained, poorly equipped and hastily gathered Eastern Fleet. There can be little doubt that a Japanese victory in such a battle would have enabled them to sweep across into Madagascar with its Vichy French ports, then on towards South Africa where they could link up with German forces in North Africa. But fate intervened and as the four R-class battleships were short of water, Somerville had to return to Addu Atoll and conflict was spared.

Meanwhile, it was accepted that some of the Intelligence was flawed and mistakes had been made. With a Japanese attack still believed to be imminent, Admiral Layton ordered all defences to go to general quarters from 3am on 5th April. Most of the ships stationed at either Colombo or Trincomalee were already at sea so those that remained were ordered to clear the harbour.

It was 8am on Easter Sunday, and an air of calm and tranquillity hung over Ceylon as the church bells rang out calling worshippers to the service but unbeknown to them, radar stations at Colombo had picked up an early warning of the first wave of incoming Japanese aircraft. The message was not delivered until 7.40am, twenty minutes before the attack began with a force of 315 fighters, bombers and attack planes. The pilots had been instructed by Vice-Admiral Nagumo not to make the mistake they had made at Pearl Harbour but to target naval harbour installations and oil tanks, as well as ships. This raid was not to be a repetition of the earlier ones on Pearl Harbour or Port Darwin. Lessons had been learned and for the first time the Japanese pilots faced stiff opposition as the incoming aircraft were met by a concentrated barrage of anti-aircraft gunfire and twenty-eight British fighters who engaged them in a short, sharp dogfight. Six Zeros were shot down at the cost of twenty RAF aircraft. As the bombers and attack planes sought their targets, fourteen Hurricanes from the racecourse airstrip attacked them. One formation of Japanese aircraft bombed shipping in and around the harbour whilst a second formation swept in at a low altitude to attack the rail yards, shops and known airfields. By 8.35am the raid was over. The British sent Blenheim bombers to counter-attack the Japanese carriers but failed to do so.

CHAPTER 4

The Events of Easter 1942

By midnight on 2nd April 1942 Vice-Admiral Nagumo was well into the Indian Ocean with the coast of Sumatra some 500 miles away. He was proceeding on a course that would take him directly to Ceylon which, if maintained, would have taken him straight to the position predicted by Admiral Somerville. He was in no hurry and steamed slowly ahead. He had already decided to delay his attack from the 4th to the 5th April, Easter Sunday, because he thought it was more likely the Eastern Fleet would be in port and Ceylon's defences less alert as it was a Sunday. It was much the same tactic as he had adopted at Pearl Harbour. During the morning of 3rd April, Nagumo refuelled his fleet, then altered course to a westerly direction and increased his speed to 20 knots. This would bring him to a flying position 160 miles to the south-west of Somerville's expectation and 200 miles from Colombo. As Nagumo was carefully positioning his fleet on 4th April, ready for the attack, Somerville and his Force A ships were entering the lagoon at Addu Atoll 600 miles away.

Working in co-operation with Nagumo on the Ceylon raids was Vice-Admiral Ozawa with the Second Expeditionary Fleet, or the Malaya Force, from Mergui, Burma, 200 miles south of Rangoon. He was waiting for Nagumo in the Bay of Bengal where his role was to destroy any merchant shipping he came across and also to attack India's east coast installations, whilst Nagumo had the more vital role of finding and destroying the British fleet. He hoped to repeat the

Vice-Admiral Ozawa.

success he had achieved at Pearl Harbour, but as will be seen, our timely intelligence prevented it.

The main body of Ozawa's fleet consisted of three elements – a Central Force consisting of one heavy cruiser, one light cruiser, one light carrier (the *Ryujo*) and two destroyers; a Southern Force consisting of two heavy cruisers and a destroyer; and a Northern Force also consisting of two heavy cruisers and a destroyer, with specific orders to bombard the enemy installations to the south of Calcutta and attack any Allied shipping found there. Attached to the Second Expeditionary Fleet was a Supply Force of two destroyers and protecting Ozawa's fleet, a Strike Force whose main body acted as a Cover Force whilst a Screening Force consisting of the light cruiser *Kashii,* the minelayer *Hatsukaka* and nine destroyers were charged with watching for enemy ships to the north of Andaman Island as well as offering protection to Nagumo's fleet as it withdrew from Ceylon.

On 28th March Admiral Somerville received an intelligence report telling him that a Japanese force was heading for the Indian Ocean, intending to make an aerial attack on Ceylon on about 1st April but only the size of Nagumo's force in this report proved to be accurate. He had put to sea, and for three days and two nights maintained his chosen attack and defence positions 80 miles to the south of Dondra Head, Ceylon. From there, Somerville hoped that reconnaissance

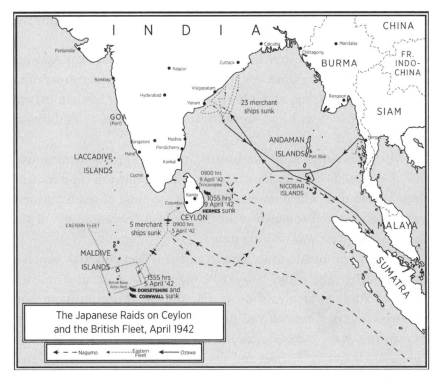

The Japanese Raids on Ceylon
and the British Fleet, April 1942

The battle plan.

aircraft would locate the Japanese strike force so that he could launch a night-time air attack from his three carriers, taking full advantage of the moonlit nights. Although his plan was sound, it was doomed to failure and on the evening of 2nd April, without having seen any Japanese ships, Somerville concluded that either his information about the strike date was wrong or Nagumo was trying to catch him unawares at night whilst his ships were at anchor. This latter option was highly likely, but it later transpired that Nagumo was not trying to outwit Somerville but was steadily making his approach as planned, to the south of Ceylon on a westerly course. Somerville's Intelligence Chiefs had merely got the date too early. As previously mentioned had Somerville been able to remain in his chosen waiting position, the two forces would have inevitably met in battle with results that could not have been anything but disastrous for the ill-trained, poorly equipped and hastily assembled Eastern Fleet.

Writing about this later in his book *Destroyer Man*, Rear Admiral Pugsley who at the time was the Captain of one of Somerville's destroyers, the *Paladin*, said 'Our fleet, with its line of battleships, was a noble sight such as I had not seen since my days as a midshipman in 1918'.

With water supplies on the British battleships getting dangerously low, they would soon need to return to port to replenish supplies. The fleet also faced an added unseen danger in the guise of seven Japanese submarines located somewhere in the area, so concentrating all the ships in one place was inviting disaster.

Having been unable to locate the Japanese fleet and with supplies running dangerously low, Somerville ordered most of his fleet back to Addu Atoll for replenishment and the following morning sent the two cruisers, *Cornwall* and the *Dorsetshire* back to Colombo, the former for convoy escort duties and the latter to resume her refit. The light aircraft carrier, *Hermes* and the destroyer, *Vampire* were ordered to Trincomalee to resume preparations for the forthcoming British invasion of Madagascar. Somerville was having serious doubts about the reliability of the Intelligence on the Japanese movements, not only with regard to timing but also whether they were indeed in the Indian Ocean. With the fleet now divided, it would obviously be ineffective against the Japanese but as the best part of it reached Addu Atoll, a reconnaissance aircraft radioed a message in the late afternoon of 4th April saying that the Japanese fleet had been sited 360 miles south of Dondra Head, the southernmost tip of Ceylon. It looked very much like the anticipated airstrike by the Japanese would take place the following morning, 5th April. Somerville was so far away he was powerless to be able to help. Seldom can a fleet have been caught more off balance.

Japanese Intelligence had indicated that the British naval strength was fast building up in the Indian Ocean and the Bay of Bengal, so Nagumo was ordered to find and destroy it. It was said he might face more than 300 aircraft over Ceylon but this was a gross exaggeration.

Our air defences were scattered over a wide area and many of our aircraft were out-of-date and capable of only a poor performance. Nagumo, on the other hand, had a massive modern strike force of 300 aircraft under his immediate command. Wherever it struck, the British could only put up at the very most, one-tenth of the Japanese numbers. Nagumo expected to find the British fleet at Trincomalee or Colombo, or if not, in the waters around Ceylon at the most 100 to 150 miles away. Reconnaissance aircraft meticulously and thoroughly searched the area. He was confident he could locate the ships and destroy them. If only the Japanese had protracted the course upon which the *Cornwall* and the *Dorsetshire* were steaming when attacked, they would have come across the ships they were seeking.

Flying his flag aboard the aircraft carrier *Akagi*, Nagumo's fleet included the carriers *Shokaku, Zuikaku, Hiryu*, and *Soryu*, each carrying a complement of between 36 and 54 light bombers and 18 Zero fighters; four battle ships, *Kongo, Hiei, Kirishima*, and *Haruna*; heavy cruisers *Tone* and *Chikums*; light cruiser *Abukama*; and eleven destroyers. There were also seven submarines operating in the Indian Ocean at the time. In terms of numbers and tonnages, Nagumo's supremacy was not so great except in the crucial matter of aircraft and aircraft carriers where he was in a totally commanding situation. Somerville decided that the only offensive action he could realistically adopt would be a night torpedo attack. It would have to be undertaken by his Fleet Air Arm Units whose practical range in Swordfish and Albacore aircraft was less than 200 miles.

For long-range reconnaissance the RAF's Catalina flying boats were ideal as they were capable of up to thirty hours flying time. However due to the need for overhauling and maintenance after their long flight to Ceylon, only one of the No.240 Squadron Catalinas was serviceable. That single Catalina was L for Lima whose captain was Flight-Lieut. W. Bradshaw, DFC; his No.2 was Pilot Officer Charles Gardner, a one-time well-known BBC broadcaster. They flew an extended search eastwards for sixteen hours but found nothing. It was a massive area for one aircraft to cover but reinforcements arrived just in time in the form of No.413 (Canadian) Squadron under the leadership of Squadron-Leader L.J. Birchall on 2nd April. The Squadron had come from the Shetland Islands in the north of Scotland and needed time to familiarize themselves with dusk and night landings on the lake at Koggala but there was an overriding urgency to find the Japanese fleet.

Squadron Leader L.J. Birchall, the 'Saviour of Ceylon'

At 6am on 4th April, with a maximum fuel load designed to keep the aircraft airborne right through until daylight on the 5th, Birchall took off with orders to patrol an area some 250 miles southeast of the island. Because of strict radio silence our own fleet's movements were not known so Birchall was told to report on all ships seen, no matter whether friendly or hostile. They searched an empty sea for hour upon hour; normal shipping lanes were far away. They continued their search to its southernmost point of almost 350 miles south-southeast of Ceylon, much further south than an enemy approach would normally be considered likely. Having been in the air for ten hours, Birchall and his crew began to work out a course back to base when they noticed a small speck on the southern horizon. With plenty of fuel still aboard, they went to investigate. It was to be a chance observation that changed the course of history.

It was surprising to find any ship in this position and at first it was thought likely to be a Royal Navy vessel but as they got closer, flying at a height of 2,000 feet, they found it was part of a large group of battleships, carriers, destroyers and supply ships. It was the Japanese fleet. Birchall flung his Catalina northwards at full boost but he was spotted and six Zeros were flown off the *Hiryu* to deal with him. The slow, heavy flying boat was no match for these aircraft. Regulations required that radio messages be repeated three times but radio operator Sgt Phillips had hardly started his second repeat when the Zeros struck. A cannon shell hit the radio set, completely destroying it whilst another shattered the leg of Sgt Calorossi, one of the blister gunners. The Japanese knew they must destroy the flying boat as quickly as possible

Sqdn. Leader Birchall.

before the fleet's presence was reported. The attack was intense and with a couple of fires breaking out on board and several of the crew badly injured, the Catalina started to break up in mid-air. Birchall fought on, taking evasive action as best as he could. They were still 350 miles from land and darkness was falling.

Back in Ceylon Birchall's message had been received, a little garbled, but basically coherent. It was immediately passed on to all the services but despite an all-night listening watch being kept for Birchall and his crew, nothing more was heard from them. When they did not return to Koggala at dawn, as expected, they were presumed to have been shot down, their fate unknown.

It later transpired, after being shot down, Squadron Leader Birchall and his crew, three of them seriously injured, had been taken aboard the destroyer *Isokaze* and held securely in the forward paint locker. Back in Ceylon it was not known for about a year what fate had befallen Birchall and his crew and he later described the incident. "As the Zeros flew in and started to attack, the Catalina began to break up in the air. Due to our flying at a low altitude it was impossible to bail out but I managed to get the aircraft down on to the water before the tail fell off. All the time we were landing and immediately thereafter we were under constant enemy strafing." At this stage the three men on the flight deck of the Catalina, Birchall, Flying Officer Kenny the second pilot and Onyette the navigator had all escaped serious injury but back in the central fuselage section, the crew had suffered badly.

The Catalina was carrying a larger crew than normal, two of whom had no formal training as air crew but who had come along as air gunners. They were Sergeant Cook, a Flight Mechanic, and Sergeant Henzell, a Flight Rigger. Apart from Sergeant Phillips, wounded as he transmitted details of the all-important sighting, Sergeant Calorossi, one of the Wireless Operators, was also badly injured whilst firing one of the guns. Of his injuries, Sergeant Catlin, the Engineer, later said, "During the action I was only aware of being hit once, in the chest, though on my left hand only the little finger still worked." Afterwards somebody counted seventy-four holes in his body.

Once down on the water, the Zeros did not let up in their attack. It was here that many of the Catalina's crew received their worst injuries. Cook and Kenny struggled to get the badly injured Henzell out of the front gun turret and in so doing Cook's leg was shattered by a burst of cannon fire. Abandoning the aircraft in such conditions was a nightmare. Calorossi, mortally wounded, was ordered out but he and Henzell went down with the aircraft. The remaining seven swam away from the blazing debris but even then the Japanese continued strafing them, according to Birchall. Their only escape was to dive beneath the waves whenever a plane approached. Sergeant Davidson was wearing a fully inflated life jacket, which made it almost impossible for him to dive. This is probably why he was hit and killed in the water. Until then it was thought he was not wounded. The remaining six stayed together and waited until the *Isokaze* picked them up.

Birchall later said he thought the main reason why the Japanese had stopped to pick them up was not out of compassion but to find out whether they had managed to send a warning signal back to Ceylon, and to obtain information about the island's defences. Birchall denied having had time to transmit a radio message and having arrived at Colombo only the day before and taken off at night, had absolutely no knowledge of Ceylon's defences. The Japanese did not believe his story as they had been listening on the correct wavelength and knew that a message had been sent. Whether they understood the code is doubtful and no one could be sure that the transmission had been picked up or even understood in Ceylon. The airmen stuck to their story but when Colombo called up and asked for clarification of the message, the beatings meted out to the captives were intensified. The airmen were dragged off to the forward paint locker, regardless that some of them had horrific injuries, where there was only room for three men to lie down at any one time; two could sit and one had to stand. Birchall's crew was kept in these inhumane conditions, with no medical attention offered and only one cup of soup a day, for the next three days. Clearly Japan did not subscribe to the requirements or niceties of the 1929 Geneva Convention, which laid down rules for the humane treatment of prisoners of war, despite her representatives having signed it, but no ratification ever followed.

Birchall and his crew were transferred to the aircraft carrier *Akagi* on 7th April where the injured men finally received medical treatment. Their new accommodation was little better than before as they were thrown into an aircraft repair well at the bottom of which was a tarpaulin. They were given blankets and pillows but kept under the glare of strong lights day and night. Later, when the *Akagi* came under attack by our Blenheims, Birchall said what with the noise of the aircraft engines revving up and the general din going on all around, he was completely unaware that bombs had been dropped close by. It was the Japanese who later told their prisoners of the attack but lied that all the aircraft had been shot down.

But crucially the Japanese had lost the vital element of surprise and this gave sufficient time for Ceylon's defences to be brought to a state of readiness.

Upon receiving Birchall's sighting report on the evening of the 4th April Admiral Somerville began steaming eastwards with those of his ships that were ready to move. It is difficult to say what his motives were in taking this course of action. If they were aggressive, the report of the impending attack on Colombo early on the 5th, particularly with regard to its great strength, had been confirmed in the garbled message received from Birchall the previous evening, but Birchall had not had the time to give details of the enemy fleet's composition.

Somerville must have realized that it would be foolhardy to confront the Japanese with a depleted fleet but perhaps he thought, even though it was impossible for him to intercept the Japanese before the attack, he just might have a chance of catching them as they withdrew, which he anticipated would be to the east.

It was imperative that the Eastern Fleet be kept intact because the defence of the Indian Ocean area and the ultimate hope of regaining control of the sea around India and Ceylon depended upon it. As it happened, perhaps fortunately in some respects, the fleet could not be brought into action either before or during the air attack on Colombo. Instead, it was fervently hoped that the Blenheim bombers based in Ceylon might be able to put one or more of the Japanese ships out of action because everyone knew that the aircraft from Somerville's carriers were not fit to deliver an effective attack by day on such a powerful enemy with its umbrella of modern fighter aircraft. Somerville's only hope was to launch a night attack with torpedo-carrying aircraft.

Somerville had learned by now that the Japanese also had a squadron consisting of one light carrier, six cruisers and four destroyers under the command of Vice-Admiral Ozawa in the Bay of Bengal. It was roaming unchallenged, sinking ships, mostly merchantmen, at will and completely disrupting sea communications on the east coast of India. The whole scenario pointed to an invasion of Ceylon and India, in conjunction with the drive through Burma. A defeat now would so damage the Allied situation that Somerville was compelled to consider the safety of his fleet as his primary objective. But Somerville, through no fault of his own, was caught out and faced a dilemma. He was 600 miles from the enemy with a fleet that had empty fuel and water tanks. Most of the ships in his fast squadron, except for the cruisers *Enterprise* and *Emerald* which could not be ready until midnight, could sail almost at once, but Force B, the four older R-class battleships that had been designed for short-range work in colder climates, could not be made ready until the next day. Conditions on these ageing battleships was said to be appalling; their steel hulls made it oppressively hot on board, especially when closed-up for action. At best, the most speed they could

HMS Dorsetshire.

manage was eighteen knots and at such a speed their fuel would last for only three or four days. With no water tankers at Addu Atoll they had to put to sea short of water, but they were unable to distil fresh water fast enough when steaming at full speed to replace boiler losses. Even before their fuel ran out, their fresh water supplies would be exhausted, despite imposing strict rationing. Maintaining morale and fighting efficiency under such conditions taxed the leadership powers of any officer to the utmost. It was agreed it would have been unwise to risk any of the fleet in the defence of Colombo.

Earlier the cruisers *Dorsetshire* and *Cornwall* had berthed at Colombo for new ack-ack, or anti-aircraft, guns and radar equipment to be fitted. *Dorsetshire*'s engineers had started to dismantle the engines for the second time in less than a week when they were told to stop work as the ship had to rejoin the main fleet immediately. Meanwhile Admiral Somerville aboard *Warspite*, together with two carriers and a few of the faster vessels of the fleet, left Addu Atoll at midnight heading eastwards towards the anticipated Japanese position.

Although Somerville had a naval force under his command which was much larger than anyone else during the war, he was far from satisfied with it. He reported back to the Admiralty in London that he was particularly dissatisfied by the lack of training shown by all his officers and men. Great things had been expected of this new fleet but Somerville was adamant he could do nothing with it until the fleet

HMS Warspite.

was fully trained. He is reported in MacIntyre's *Fighting Admiral* as having said, 'The trouble is, the fleet I now have is much bigger than anything anyone has had to handle before or during this war. Everyone is naturally very rusty about doing their "fleet stuff" – most ships have hardly been in company with another ship during the war. On top of all that, most of my staff are pretty green, so I have to supervise almost everything myself. It will improve as time goes on but it certainly is the devil of a job at present.'

He was also equally damning in his appraisal of the pilots under his command. When mustering his fleet on 31st March he described it as "collecting all my scattered and untrained boys to see what I can do about it". Nonetheless he maintained an unfailingly optimistic attitude towards his troops and still managed to boost their morale at a time when it needed boosting. Somerville had built up his reputation in the Mediterranean fighting the Italians. It was strange to hear his derogatory remarks about his new fleet but perhaps they had only been meant for their Lordships at the Admiralty. It hardly seems feasible that the fleet could have been so untrained, especially as the war had been going on for two and a half years. But whatever the fleet's shortcomings, it was now the turn of Ceylon's air defences to prove their mettle.

It was now believed the Japanese would attack Ceylon early the next morning so in order to regain contact with the Japanese fleet to confirm this, Flight-Lieut. Graham in a No.205 Squadron Catalina was sent to shadow it, using the sighting position radioed in by Squadron. Leader Birchall as a starting point. Sometime between midnight and 1am he signalled that he had sighted an enemy destroyer some 200 miles to the southeast of Ceylon. The message was not repeated and no further word was ever heard from Graham or his crew.

With Graham's Catalina having failed to return, presumed to have been shot down like Birchall's, there was still a pressing need to maintain a watch on the Japanese fleet but the Allied Chiefs of Staff were reluctant to commit a third Catalina, knowing it too would probably be lost. It had to done however, and Flt-Lieut. Bradshaw DFC of No. 240 Squadron was detailed to take up the search in order to regain contact. Flying at low level to avoid detection by Japanese radar – Bradshaw was unaware that the Japanese had none – he saw in the distance a large number of aircraft flying northwards at a greater altitude than him. Having been briefed to expect seeing carrier-borne aircraft in the area and assuming them to be friendly due to their close proximity to Ceylon, Bradshaw did not break radio silence to report their presence. The Japanese pilots did not spot Bradshaw either as he was flying so low. Soon, Bradshaw spotted the Japanese fleet's forward elements; they were the battleships and cruisers which had moved protectively ahead of the carriers. As he headed for home Bradshaw radioed in his sighting report.

At first light on Easter Sunday, 5th April two routine patrols flew out, one consisting of two Hurricanes from No.30 Squadron, and the other, six Fleet Air Arm Fulmars. They flew just below the cloud line in battle formation keeping an eye open for the Japanese fleet and on their way back to base the Fulmars actually spotted some of the enemy aircraft.

There had been several thoughts as to when the attack might be expected. Some thought a dawn attack was likely but that would mean a difficult night take-off from the carriers. In view of the known position of the Japanese fleet, such an attack would be more likely on the following day, 6th April. Others suggested that if the enemy aircraft took off at dawn, they would arrive at Ceylon at about 8am. Whilst the bombers could easily manage this distance, it was too far for the Zero fighters and it would have been foolhardy for the bombers to attack without fighter support, a step considered to be too rash even for the Japanese. A third school of thought suggested that in order to utilize fighter protection, the Japanese fleet would have to steam closer to get within normal fighter range. If this were the chosen option then the attack could be expected nearer midday. On the airfields all the aircrews could do was to watch and wait.

Out at sea on Admiral Somerville's flagship, a disturbing number of signals started to come in from merchant ships hugging the eastern coastline of India as one ship after another reported being attacked by aircraft or surface vessels. It looked like the action was about to begin.

Two hundred miles south of Ceylon at daybreak, Nagumo's fleet of five aircraft carriers, four fast battleships, three cruisers and eight destroyers, was steaming as close as he dared and having reached the designated take-off area, the first of his aircraft roared into the sky. The force of 180 aircraft was under the command of Commander Mitsuo Fuchida of the *Akagi* who had led the attack on Pearl Harbour. He was one of Japan's most experienced flyers who already had 25 years service in the Imperial Navy. He was by far the oldest man to be flying on either side that day. The Japanese pilots took off in quick succession from the five carriers as they steamed into the wind and headed for Colombo. Fuchida was certain the Catalina had had time to radio back a report giving details of the Japanese position and that Ceylon's defences had been brought to a state of readiness. Until the previous day the element of surprise had still been with them and they had no reason to believe they were expected. They had hoped to achieve the same element of surprise as they had had at Pearl Harbour but now realized their plan was in jeopardy. Stiff opposition was to be expected.

Meanwhile, operating separately from their carrier force, the Japanese battleships and cruisers launched their seaplanes at dawn to conduct a wide-ranging search to the west and the south for a distance of 250 miles, looking for the Eastern Fleet in case it was not in Colombo harbour as Nagumo expected it would be. This was the part of the

Commander Fuchida.

fleet that Flight-Lieut. Bradshaw had spotted a few minutes after he had seen the Japanese strike force pass high overhead.

Fuchida's force consisted of 54 Type 99 dive bombers (Vals), each with a crew of three, 90 Type 97 attack bombers (Kates), each with a crew of three and an escort of 36 Zero fighters. Fuchida himself flew as an observer in one of the Kates, which was piloted by Lieut. Mitsuo Matsuzaki. After take-off the aircraft climbed steadily on a course for the southwest coast of Ceylon. The plan was, after making landfall, to fly well clear of the coastline, northwards towards the capital. The fact that the Zero was capable of flying over 200 miles, spending twenty minutes in the combat zone, then returning the same distance, was totally unexpected by the Allies. It was a long flight for any pilot to make and the Allies had no comparable aircraft. For this particular mission the Zeros carried auxiliary fuel tanks which were jettisoned shortly before arriving at Colombo.

A Zero taking off from the *Akagi*.

Ceylon had limited radar cover with only one unit, No.524 AMES having been set up just a few days previously, but exercises and practice raids carried out over the past few weeks had shown it was sufficient to ensure the defences would have adequate warning. Reinforcements were on their way but at the time of the impending attack were still in convoy. Ceylon's modest radar coverage and the radar posts were linked by commandeered telephone lines to Fighter Operations Headquarters in Colombo, but incredibly, the radar posts were not manned when the Japanese force crossed the coastline south of Colombo. There are various stories about them being shut down for maintenance, as was normal on a Sunday, or there was a rather relaxed shift change but both accounts are bizarre.

Whether radar picked up the incoming Japanese aircraft or not is immaterial as the British Hurricanes could have been given at least half an hour's warning from visual sightings alone. This enormous battle formation was actually spotted by six Fulmars of No. 803 Squadron that were on regular patrol that day at 2,000 ft. between Ratmalana and the east coast. Sub. Lieut. R.V. Hinton reported how on the return journey, somewhere between Bentota and Colombo, his pilots saw a number of aircraft out to sea, some distance away, but it did not occur to them at the time that they were Japanese aircraft. It subsequently transpired that as the first bombs fell on Ratmalana, the radio network went dead, though not through direct enemy action, and consequently the aircraft were not in communication with their base. If communication had been maintained, Hinton was confident he could have got his aircraft into an attacking position as the Japanese withdrew from Ceylon. But as it was, no one on the west coast had any reason to believe the incoming aircraft were anything but friendly.

It has never been satisfactorily explained why Fighter Operations did not learn of the Japanese aircraft's arrival until after No.30 Squadron had been engaged and No.258 was taking off from the racecourse airstrip. It has been suggested the watches were being changed at the crucial moment and the radar had been unmanned for some time.

In mitigation, since no one realized the great range of the Japanese aircraft, the radar operators believed the carriers would need to get much closer to Ceylon and the attack would therefore take place later in the day.

And so on Easter Sunday 1942, St Luke's Church in Borella was packed for the Easter services with both locals and military personnel when the action began. According to parishioners, the vicar, Rev Canon Ivan Corea, was preaching when the RAF Hurricanes started engaging the Japanese Zero aircraft high above the church and the Sri Lankan writer Ariyadasa Ratnasinghe recalled the Easter Sunday raid by saying, "Japanese aircraft flew in close formation over Colombo and dropped bombs at different places. The air battle lasted for nearly half an hour. The Allied forces, warned of the danger, were able to shoot down some of the enemy aircraft which fell on land and sea." At Ratmalana the early morning sun had risen high in the sky and there was no indication of an impending attack. Some felt it was another false alarm and at 7.30am some of the men were sent to have their breakfast. Twenty minutes later the first Japanese formations roared overhead, taking everyone by surprise.

Despite their long vigil No.30 Squadron under Squadron Leader G.F. Chater DFC was caught out on the ground by the Japanese and with over 8,000 ft. to climb before reaching the enemy bombers, they knew it would be suicidal trying to fight their way up through the escorting fighter aircraft screen which was already in a far superior position. We now know that one advantage the Hurricane had over the Zero was that through its greater weight, it could out-dive the Zero. But at this time we were faced with the simple fact that any aircraft, no matter how superior or inferior it might be to an enemy aircraft, it is at its most vulnerable point just after take-off before full power can be built up or speed and altitude gained.

The Japanese strike force had made its landfall at 7.15am in the Galle area over Colombo's Marine Parade and flown on up the coast for half an hour at a height of 8,000 ft. In accordance with Vice-Admiral Nagumo's orders not to repeat the mistakes made at Pearl Harbour or Port Darwin, the Japanese pilots headed for the naval harbour installations and oil depots at Kolonnawa to the east of the city. One formation attacked the ships in and around the harbour whilst the second, Fuchida's Type 97 attack bombers, came in low and strafed the rail yards at Ratmalana, the shopping areas, and the racecourse airfield, as well as bombing them. This initial attack was followed by high altitude bombing aimed at the few ships that remained in the harbour being repaired, causing the sinking of the destroyer *Tenedos* and an armed merchant cruiser, the *Hector*, as well as severely damaging a submarine tender, the *Lucia* and a freighter. The naval repair shops were totally destroyed but mercifully the port of Colombo was not put out of action.

Meanwhile, at the racecourse airstrip No.258 Squadron had little warning of the actual attack. Fighter Operations phoned the C.O., Squadron Leader P.C. Fletcher asking if anything was known of the enemy force and Fletcher is alleged to have answered, "Yes, they are right overhead now and we are taking off". The Mark IIB Hurricanes had been adapted for use in the tropics and were fitted with the more
• powerful two-stage supercharged Rolls Royce Merlin XX engine giving them an extra 20 mph over the Mark I used in the desert campaign. Another improvement was they now carried twelve guns instead of the usual eight, but in order to lighten the aircraft and improve its performance, Fletcher had four of the guns taken out.

Squadron Leader Fletcher took off first, leading the attack. Three minutes later New Zealander, Flight Lieutenant 'Denny' Sharp took off in one of the Mark Is. He was one of the few of our airmen who had any experience in fighting the Japanese. As No.258 Squadron's Hurricanes left the runway the Japanese strike force was directly overhead, flying inland over Colombo in several loose formations with the intention of making their attack from the landward side.

As the Japanese turned to start their bombing run they spotted six Swordfish biplanes armed with torpedoes beneath them, strung out in line astern, approaching the city from the north. These old biplanes were Lieut. Longsdon's "Stringbags", which had unfortunately arrived over Colombo on their way to Ratmalana from Trincomalee at the very moment the Japanese were launching their attack. Their orders had been to refuel, then proceed to attack the enemy fleet. Regulations stipulated that friendly aircraft approaching Colombo should fly in through a recognized corridor from the north at a slow speed, at a height of 2,000 ft. and to break formation by flying in line astern instead. Despite making it clear that any aircraft flying in this predetermined way were friendly, it put the aircraft in a vulnerable position in the event of a surprise attack. At first the six Fleet Air Arm pilots were not perturbed as the fighters approached them; they were used to RAF Hurricanes coming up to take a look at them. Fuchida called up Lieut-Commander Shigeru Itaya who was leading the fighter wing and ordered him to deal with the Swordfish. Interestingly Itaya, another of Nagumo's senior officers, had had a hand in the final design of the Zero back in 1938 when he was second in command of the Yokasuka Experimental Air Corps.

Unaware of the situation unfolding before them, Sub-Lieut. Mackay, Longsdon's observer, flashed the code letter of the day, "N" and Leading Airman Skingley, in Sub-Lieut. Meakin's aircraft, fired the recognition signal of two green stars. To everyone's dismay the leading fighter turned in to attack, followed at five-second intervals by the other five aircraft, all of which opened fire from a distance of about 600 yards with deadly accuracy. The Swordfish took what evasive action they could but were hampered in that they were carrying torpedoes. There was scarcely time for any sort of defence but a couple of the Swordfish rear gunners did manage to bring their guns to bear for a few rounds but unfortunately with little effect. Most of the biplanes were hit in the first attack and their crews injured. A second attack swiftly followed and all six Swordfish were sent crashing to the ground. Not satisfied with downing the aircraft, the Zeros then swept in for a third time to strafe any survivors. Of the fourteen men involved in this attack, five were killed and five badly wounded. Lieut. Longsdon was badly wounded and his aircraft ended up upside down in a paddy field.

With the Japanese now over Ratmalana airstrip all haste was made to get its aircraft airborne and 19 Hurricanes and 12 Fulmars succeeded in getting away. They fell easy prey to the Zeros and in a short space of time 8 of the Hurricanes and 4 of the Fulmars were shot down with the Japanese loosing only 4 Vals. Over at the racecourse airfield, which was not known about by the Japanese, 14 Hurricanes had taken off and climbed undetected to make an attack from out of cloud cover. Between them they shot down 2 Vals, but made the fatal mistake of engaging with the highly manoeuvrable Zeros in dogfights and lost 9 aircraft.

Meanwhile, some of the pilots of No.30 Squadron had managed to get airborne and had joined No.258 Squadron in the fray. By not knowing of the existence of the racecourse airstrip, once Ratmalana had been dealt with the Japanese pilots anticipated supremacy in the air but they failed to notice the Hurricanes of No.258 Squadron coming up to meet them. This was the Squadron that accounted for many of the attackers. Squadron Leader Fletcher later recounted the action. "After clawing for height, there was a lot of lumpy cloud about, but quite good visibility in between. I had clearly seen the tight formation of the Jap bombers, with fighters above them, heading inland. I decided they would turn and attack the harbour from the landside.

"We did a climbing turn towards the harbour; I was still hoping against hope to get above them but if not, a head-on attack against the formation might be possible. Suddenly a couple of Jap bombers dived down through a gap in the clouds, very close to us. Obviously dive-bomber attacks had started. We were still much below the bombers so I had a difficult decision to make. It looked as if we had been spotted. There was (sic) masses of cloud cover about and if we continued climbing, we might get the precious height we needed. On the other hand, by that time the bombers would have done a lot of damage; we would be seen by the Zeros sooner or later and would be mixing it with them instead of getting at the bombers.

"I decided to go after the bombers, shouted "Tally-ho" and turned into a dive through a cloud between us and the gap through which the Japanese were diving. Some of the formation lost me in the cloud but two or three were still with me when we broke cloud and were in a good position to attack. From then on it was every man for himself."

Squadron Leader Fletcher was somewhat angered to see the anti-aircraft gun batteries below still firing in his direction amongst the Japanese planes. As he was positioning his aircraft to open fire on an enemy bomber he both heard and felt a heavy 'thud' just below him. Quickly looking around, he could not see any Zeros. It was a shell-burst from one of our own guns. Oil and fumes entered the cockpit and as he turned for home, whilst at the same time checking his cockpit to see how serious things were, Fletcher felt some 'cracking bangs' into the back of his seat and a twinge of pain in his shoulder. Two Zeros were right behind him. He went into a steep turn, applying full power, and oil gushed into the cockpit. He bailed out but whilst floating down to earth the two Zeros took it in turn to fire at the helpless pilot. He played dead and eventually landed unscathed in a coconut plantation near a small temple where one of the Zeros still pursued him. Both Fletcher and his No.2, fellow Rhodesian Flight-Lieut. S.R. Peacock-Edwards, were awarded the DFC for their part in the battle.

Flight-Lieut. Peacock-Edwards similarly recorded his memories of this battle. He was a veteran of the Advanced Air Striking Force which had moved into France at the outbreak of war, as well as the Battle of Britain and Malta. He recalled how after being scrambled his formation climbed up towards the enemy, then swept round over the harbour where the Japanese aircraft were concentrated, and out to sea. Flying at a height of about 4,000 ft. just out to sea from the harbour, the Japanese who by this time were just behind and slightly above the British aircraft, passed by Peacock-Edwards' formation which was still climbing at maximum boost. They broke their formation and started to dive-bomb the harbour and its shipping – what little there was of it.

Peacock-Edwards questions whether the Japanese pilots even saw the British planes because they dived straight through the middle of them. The British attacked with intensity and a dog-fight ensued, during which Peacock-Edwards shot down one Navy 99, or Val, dive-bomber, but was soon set upon by enemy fighters which he managed to shake off by climbing. Two more pursued him and when he got himself into a superior position, attacked the one he considered to be in the most vulnerable position. Peacock-Edwards recalled how he followed this aircraft down but did not see the result of his attack because he himself was then set upon by half a dozen fighter aircraft.

To escape from his attackers Peacock-Edwards adopted a hide and seek tactic amongst the many palm trees. Being at such a low altitude was a distinct disadvantage for his Hurricane but he had no choice. Four of the Zeros held back at a safe height whilst the other two buzzed around like angry bees, alternating between head-on and stern attacks. Peacock-Edwards managed to get some bursts of canon fire into the Zeros during their head-on attacks but could not see where. He was sure the aircraft were damaged and possibly did not make it back to their carrier but he could not say so with any certainty.

Finally he was forced to crash-land in a paddy field. Dazed and sitting amidst the wreckage, Peacock-Edwards was aware of a Zero circling overhead but it made no effort to attack him until he clambered out in case a fire broke out. As he clawed his way through the mud of the paddy field, heading for cover nearby, the Zero made a half-hearted attack but it was futile and Peacock-Edwards made his way safely back to the racecourse airstrip.

Some of the Fulmars of No.803 and No.806 Squadrons based at Ratmalana had also taken off and joined the battle. Four were lost and one was shot down as it was coming in to land. The Fulmar was basically a two-seater reconnaissance aircraft that had the performance of the Japanese Navy 97 bomber, which it closely resembled in appearance. As a fighter aircraft the Fulmar was not only much slower but was out-manoeuvred and was no match against the Zeros. As one Fulmar pilot later commented, "The only way we could mix it with the Japs was to dive from a great height from out of the sun, have a go, and get the hell out of it." These optimum conditions unfortunately did not prevail on the day as the Japanese were already flying at 10,000 ft. and the Fulmar was a slow climber even at full boost. As soon as the results of the Easter Sunday battle had been studied, it was decided the

A Fleet Air Arm Fulmar.

Fulmar should never be used as a fighter again but when later another air battle raged over Ceylon, the Fulmars once again went gallantly into action, after all, in a battle, anything's better than nothing. And Admiral Layton was most disparaging when in a report to the Admiralty he said, 'Fleet Air Arm aircraft are proving more of an embarrassment than a help, when landed. They cannot operate by day in the presence of Jap fighters and only tend to congest aerodromes.'

In the meantime the Zeros had rejoined the main force which was by then attacking the harbour but to their disappointment there was only one British warship, the antiquated destroyer *Tenedos*, which was undergoing a refit and was immobilized just off one of the jetties. She had been one of the four destroyers escorting the *Prince of Wales* and *Repulse* when they were sunk off Malaya and had brought back many survivors on her limited deck space. Although not recognizable as such to the Japanese there was one other vessel in the harbour that was serving under the White Ensign as an armed merchant cruiser, the *Hector* who had been escorting convoys between the Middle East, India and Australia for nearly two years. She was being decommissioned and had only a skeleton crew aboard so she could not put to sea. Together with the submarine depot ship *Lucia* these three vessels took the brunt of the Japanese attack and whilst the *Lucia* was badly damaged, the *Tenedos* and *Hector* were both sunk. A bomb blew the stern of the *Tenedos* away, an explosion made far greater by the depth-charges she had on board, and a neighbouring merchantman, the *Benledi*, which at the time was unloading motor transport and bombs, was herself struck by a bomb and severely damaged by the blast. The *Hector* settled on the bottom of the harbour and burned steadily for a fortnight, said to be one of the longest marine fires in history. Her derelict hulk remained in the centre of the harbour for the next two years, becoming a familiar landmark until she was raised and beached a few miles away to the north, out of the way. One of those killed on the *Tenedos* was Ordinary Seaman Sir Robert Peel, Bt, son of the music hall comedienne Beatrice Lillie.

At the time of the attack lady luck must have been smiling on No.11 Squadron whose Blenheims had been moved to the racecourse airstrip just over a week earlier. Had they still been at Ratmalana the Japanese pilots would surely have spotted them. As the attack began Wing Commander A.J.M. Smyth, DFC was preparing to lead ten Blenheims with a payload of 500 lb semi-armour piercing bombs to seek out the enemy fleet, using Bradshaw's sighting point from which to calculate their likely position. With No.258 Squadron's Hurricanes monopolizing the runway and so many enemy aircraft overhead, take-off was out of the question, but they finally got away at 8.30am. Once airborne the Blenheims flew southwards, assuming the Japanese would have turned south from the point where Flight-Lieut. Bradshaw's Catalina had sighted them earlier that morning. However, Wing-Commander Smyth must have flown too far to the east as he missed the fleet altogether and returned to Colombo at 2.30pm, his mission unfulfilled. It can only be assumed the Blenheims must have passed between the two fleets but could see neither due to thick cloud cover. A medium bomber such as the Blenheim is far less useful against ships than a torpedo bomber, even more so if it does not have a fighter escort, and although the chances of No.11 Squadron causing any serious damage to the Japanese fleet were slender without the risk of being shot down themselves, their failure to locate the enemy was a bitter blow.

By the end of the battle, No.30 Squadron could muster only seven serviceable aircraft so if the Japanese had resumed their offensive straightaway they would have been hopelessly outnumbered. Back at the racecourse airstrip, of the fourteen Hurricanes that had taken off, nine had not returned. Five pilots had been killed and others injured whilst bailing out of their stricken aircraft. No.258 Squadron could muster only nine aircraft. Together with the Fleet Air Arm we had lost 27 aircraft over Colombo with 17 airmen killed and 11 injured.

At the time we claimed to have destroyed 27 enemy aircraft, a claim met with great rejoicing as this was the first claim to be made against the Japanese. Until this moment in time it had been the Japanese who had been triumphant in conquering all they came into contact with. In actuality only three Japanese aircraft were shot down over Ceylon and the Japanese themselves admitted to loosing five although the other two could well have crashed into the sea on their retreat back to the carriers. Had they been damaged in the action it is unlikely they could have made the long flight back. This was later confirmed by Fuchida. Furthermore, it was said the enemy 'had been driven off', which was equally heartening after the succession of communiqués that had circulated since the Japanese offensive began.

Amongst the civilian casualties incurred that day, one bomb fell short of its intended target and damaged the Angoda mental hospital, killing seven of its inmates and injuring many others. It is thought the bomb was intended for the nearby Kolonnawa oil refinery. Another bomb fell near the Maradana railway station, partly damaging it, and causing many deaths and more casualties, mostly civilians. After the attack it was decided, in order to prevent bombs being dropped on hospitals in future, either intentionally or unintentionally, a large red cross would be painted on their roofs for the guidance of the pilots. Although the damage to Ceylon's railway installations caused by the high-level bombers was not extensive, it was the demoralizing effect it had on the civilian population that was much more effective. The raid had come as a complete shock since it had not been considered advisable to issue a prior warning in case it caused panic. It had lasted some twenty minutes and civilian casualties amounted to 85 dead and 77 injured. The last of the Zeros left Colombo at about 8.30am and were seen circling aimlessly just out to sea for five minutes or more, waiting no doubt for a rendezvous with the bombers that unbeknown to them, had long gone.

It was time to take stock of the situation. As the sun began to set on that Easter Sunday evening there was hope for a few hours respite from the prevailing tension and much of Colombo's population was streaming out of the city as a huge exodus began. The Ceylonese people, like many around the world, had heard rumours of the atrocities carried out against civilians by Japanese troops in China, Hong Kong and Singapore, and did not want to become the next victim. The ferry from Talaimannar to India was packed night after night. At Ratmalana and the racecourse airstrip ground crews worked feverishly to get the remaining Hurricanes into a serviceable condition. And with many experienced pilots either dead or badly wounded, the small band of survivors prepared for the next attack which was expected at any time.

Because of a general break-down in communications it was difficult for those in charge to piece together the results of this first assault on the island. Even our own air casualties could not be precisely determined straight away. The lengths some COs had to go to was astonishing. Typically, Squadron-Leader Chater had to fly from Ratmalana airport to the racecourse airstrip himself just to regain contact and see whether any of his missing Hurricanes were there instead of where they should have been because eight were missing, unaccounted for.

That evening the Governor, Sir Andrew Caldecott broadcast on Radio Ceylon, praising the civilian population for their courage and calmness. Once news of the attack on Colombo had been released it was generally thought a similar raid would follow on Madras. An air-raid warning sounded on the 7th adding fuel to the expectation and a self-imposed rapid evacuation of civilians began just as there had from Colombo. Fortunately it was a false alarm. Despite this uncertainty, the Governor of Madras, Sir Arthur Hope, ill-advisedly issued a general warning that a Japanese invasion might be imminent so Government departments began a planned evacuation programme and troops began immobilizing operations in the port and on the railways. Tension quickly spread throughout southern India.

As Fuchida was starting to break off the attack on Colombo his radio officer, Petty Officer Mizuki picked up a disturbing message transmitted to Vice-Admiral Nagumo from one of the cruiser *Tone's* seaplanes on patrol to the north-west of the Japanese fleet, saying that it appeared the British fleet were about to launch a surface attack on the Japanese ships. The likely timing of this attack would coincide with the return of his aircraft from the attack on Colombo so the carriers' decks needed to be kept clear to receive them, but at the same time the decks were needed to launch other aircraft to attack the British ships. Furthermore, Nagumo knew it would take some time to rearm his incoming aircraft with torpedoes and bombs. There must have been considerable confusion aboard the carriers. At first the seaplane reported the vessels as being two enemy destroyers heading south-southwest at a speed of 25 knots, well within the range of the Japanese bombers but later the pilot corrected his earlier message to say that the destroyers were in fact cruisers, which were of course the *Cornwall* and the *Dorsetshire*. Nagumo had retained sufficient aircraft for a second strike on Ceylon if required, but was advised by Fuchida to hold back. It was a huge disappointment for him to learn that the British fleet had not been found at Colombo and there had been only lesser targets for his bombers in the harbour.

As was later shown, Fuchida's advice was sound because after receiving the report on the two cruisers, Nagumo ordered his second bombing force, which he had held in reserve, to fly to the scene to shadow and then attack the two cruisers once reinforcements arrived. A force of 80 Val dive-bombers, led by Lieut.-Commander Takashige Egusa, Air Group Commander of the *Soryu* took off to look for the

British cruisers at 11.30am. But Fuchida's assessment of the situation was unduly pessimistic as he ordered an immediate recall of all bombers from Ceylon without waiting for them to reform, leaving his fighters to deal with No.258 Squadron's Hurricanes. These fighter aircraft had to later find their own way back to the carriers without the help of the bombers' navigators and without the benefit of the homing devices that were fitted only on the bombers. Fuchida knew he was taking a calculated risk in ordering this course of action and as was later discovered, several aircraft did not make it back to the carriers.

His pessimistic actions might be explained by the fact that his task force was divided, with the carrier force 100 miles due south of Galle when he altered course to the south-west, steering into the wind at an increased speed of 26 knots, ready to receive the returning aircraft, whilst his battleship force was some 40 miles away to the south-east which seemed unwise if he was expecting a shore-based air attack.

In the late afternoon of 5th April, just before sunset, at 16:55 and again at 18:00, two Albacores from the aircraft carriers *Formidable* and *Indomitable* made contact with the Japanese carriers. One Albacore was shot down and the other damaged before an accurate sighting report could be made, frustrating Admiral Somerville's plans for a retaliatory night strike by his ASV radar-equipped Albacore strike bombers. Somerville continued to look for the Japanese carriers throughout that night but failed to find any enemy ships, and so his only opportunity to launch a strike against the enemy faded away.

While Nagumo's carrier force had been running rings around the Eastern Fleet off Ceylon, Vice-Admiral Ozawa's cruisers had sunk twenty-three merchant ships, causing the British to suspend all shipping operations between Burma and India. It had cost over 100,000 tons in losses and convinced Somerville he had no alternative but to withdraw his fleet to the African coast at Mombasa. It was a strategic withdrawal he would certainly not have considered had he known that on that very afternoon Nagumo had set course for home. The carrier force had steamed some 50,000 miles since Pearl Harbour and Nagumo's ships were in urgent need of repair and refit.

After this latest disaster to our control of the Indian Ocean, Churchill warned President Roosevelt, "Immense perils are now threatening Burma and India". He suggested that the US Pacific Fleet should send warships to join Somerville "to offer menace to the Japanese" but Admiral Ernest King, Commander-in-Chief of the US Fleet and Chief of Naval Operations, would not hear of it. Admiral King directed the US Navy's operations, planning and administration, and was one of the Joint Chiefs of Staff, and as such, was the US Navy's second most senior officer. Roosevelt replied to Churchill's suggestion by offering to send more bombers to strengthen the defence of India. He gave no hint of an operation America already had in hand, to strike back at Japan, a plan intended largely as propaganda to boost American morale. It was to jolt the Imperial General Staff so much that it changed the course of the war in the Pacific.

CHAPTER 5

The Loss of the *Cornwall*, the *Dorsetshire* and Other Ships

Admiral Somerville's Force A left Addu Atoll at midday on 5th April, heading for a position some 250 miles south of Ceylon and expecting to be there by daybreak on the 6th. He ordered his two heavy cruisers, the *Cornwall* and the *Dorsetshire* to join him from Colombo at 1600 hrs on the 5th. However, at 0648 that morning the *Dorsetshire* heard that the Japanese were some 150 miles to her east. Both cruisers went to flank speed (ie 27½ knots for the *Cornwall*) but as visibility was clear, a seaplane from the Japanese cruiser *Tone* spotted both cruisers shortly after noon.

This seaplane was probably the reconnaissance aircraft of which Masatake Okumiya spoke of in the book *Zero. The Story of the Japanese Navy Air Force, 1937–45* which he co-wrote with Jiro Horikoshi and Martin Caidin in 1957. Okumiya had been a wartime Field Staff Officer at the Japanese Air Force HQ and was in a unique position to follow the course of the air war in the Pacific and Indian Oceans. His book, *Zero …*, is primarily the story of the Zero fighter aircraft and in it Okumiya traces its meteoric success from the early days, following Pearl Harbour, up to the time of an increasing challenge by our own carrier-based aircraft. It is obvious that Okumiya had access to the actual reports received from the Japanese carriers and the official log books of those pilots participating in the attack on the *Cornwall* and the *Dorsetshire*.

In his book Okumiya recalls how even as the raid on Colombo was still taking place, one of Nagumo's reconnaissance planes radioed a message saying the pilot had spotted two enemy destroyers heading south-south-west at a speed of 25 knots. This placed them approximately 300 nautical miles south-south-west of Colombo. Nagumo thought the destruction of these destroyers would complement his attack on Colombo, so Lieut-Commander Takashige Egusa, Air Group Commander of the *Soryu* led 80 Val dive-bombers in a hunt for them. But then Nagumo received a corrected message saying that the two destroyers were in fact cruisers. As soon as Egusa's attack force spotted the ships he radioed two short and concise messages back to Nagumo, each a few minutes apart. Photos taken at the time by the pilots identified the ships as the *Cornwall* and the *Dorsetshire*.

• Egusa's pilots had been hand-picked as an elite force, trained to destroy America's aircraft-carriers, but had been thwarted when they arrived at Pearl Harbour to find none there. As soon as they spotted the two British cruisers they divided into two groups, scoring hit after

HMS Dorsetshire.

HMS Cornwall.

hit right from the start of their attack. The line of attack had been carefully worked out in advance and the aircraft attacked in formations of three. Those manning the anti-aircraft guns were frustrated to find the bombers approaching from immediately ahead and retiring astern. Most of the guns were blind on this particular bearing to safeguard the ship's rigging and superstructure. This was a legacy of the times when one ship fought another, broadside on. The benefits of aerial warfare against ships had yet to be discovered, so a ship's armaments were positioned with this in mind.

Following the raid on Colombo, Nagumo had turned westwards and continued on that course to help Egusa's aircraft find the *Cornwall* and the *Dorsetshire*. Lieut.-Commander Takashige Egusa took off at 11.30am with 80 Type 99 dive-bombers (Vals) from the *Soryu,* the *Hiryu* and the *Akagi* and headed in the direction of the British cruisers. Each one of the Vals carried a single 250kg bomb on a ventral cradle which was swung forward and downward to clear the propeller during delivery and a 60kg bomb attached to either outer wing. After dropping its bombs the Val was sufficiently well-armed and manoeuvrable to become a fighter aircraft that could put up a creditable fight against

Allied fighters with its 7.7mm machine gun in each wing and one in the rear cockpit.

Both Captain Agar on the *Dorsetshire* and Captain Manwaring on the *Cornwall* had detected a second shadowing seaplane on their radar but as it was on the limits of the horizon, they were not unduly concerned by its presence. Both ships expected to be under the protection of air cover from the aircraft of *Formidable* and *Indomitable* by 2pm. In their estimation it was unlikely they were within the immediate range of the carrier-borne aircraft of the Japanese fleet so it came as something of a shock to discover the accepted estimated range of the Japanese aircraft was considerably wide of the mark. Erring on the side of caution, both ships' companies went to action stations and pressed on at full speed to rejoin the rest of the British fleet.

The *Dorsetshire* was slightly faster than her sister-ship *Cornwall* so she slowed down to 27½ knots (*Cornwall's* maximum) in order that the two cruisers could stay together for added protection. It was a calm day with little or no cloud, there was a slight haze over the sun and visibility was good. At about 11am a single aircraft was sighted by the lookouts of the *Cornwall*, flying about 20 miles astern but was lost from sight before it could be identified. This was reported to the *Dorsetshire*. Shortly after 1pm a number of radar contacts were picked up by both cruisers but it was thought there was a strong likelihood they were our own aircraft that both the *Cornwall* and the *Dorsetshire* had been expecting.

Until now radio silence had been observed in accordance with the orthodox principle adopted by the Royal Navy for ships at sea but on this occasion radio silence was broken to notify Admiral Somerville of the cruisers' position, to report the enemy shadowing them and the possibility of an air attack. The message was received in a mutilated form at about 2pm and was identified as coming from the *Dorsetshire* but by then, it was too late for Somerville to help; both cruisers had been sunk. Somerville immediately changed course to a southerly bearing when he heard of the threat to the two cruisers but when he later heard they had both been sunk, reversed his course in pursuit of the Japanese fleet.

At 1340hrs three aircraft were spotted by the lookouts of the *Dorsetshire*, flying at a high altitude directly overhead. Assuming them to be hostile she opened fire but within a few seconds they were seen to be diving on the *Cornwall,* a mile to port.

Simultaneously a separate formation of three aircraft attacked the *Dorsetshire.* She swung to starboard but all three bombs struck their target and by 1348hrs she had sunk; she was closely followed at about 1400hrs by the *Cornwall.* The radar aboard Somerville's flagship, *Warspite* had itself picked up the formation of Japanese aircraft at 1344hrs, flying some 84 miles away to the north-east but they posed no threat and soon faded from the screen. It was later realised this was the strike force heading for the two cruisers.

Captain Agar later commented that the reason for the Japanese success in sinking the *Dorsetshire* and the *Cornwall* was no doubt due to their clever tactics of attacking with the sun behind them (hence the shout adopted by many pilots during the Battle of Britain, 'Beware of the Hun in the Sun') and approaching the ship from ahead, the cruiser's blind spot for anti-aircraft defences. The two cruisers had unknowingly helped the Japanese pilots by being on a southerly course at the time of the attack.

Typical of this frustration at not being able to fire back at the attacking aircraft, on the *Dorsetshire* Ray Lock was manning a 'pom-pom' gun (an automatic rapid-firing, small-calibre, 20-40mm,

Cornwall and *Dorsetshire* under attack, as seen by the Japanese pilots.

anti-aircraft gun) amidships and was fuming at the hopelessly restricted field of fire. Suddenly, as a bomb struck, he was flung to the deck some ten feet below him. Shaken but appearing to be uninjured, he got to his feet intent on returning to his gun platform only to see only two black stumps remaining of what had once been the twin gun barrels. The rest of the crew in that area were either dead or badly wounded. It was only later that Ray noticed a squelching sound coming from his shoes which were filled with blood. He then realized that he was seriously wounded in the chest and legs.

The bombs fell in quick succession, accurately striking the ship's aircraft catapult, the wireless telegraph installation near the bridge, and the engine and boiler rooms. Her guns blazed away in defiance but one by one were put out of action. With her steering jammed hard to starboard, the ship swung in a wide circle until she shuddered to a halt. Suddenly there was an explosion as a bomb hit one of the magazines. The valve on the ship's siren was shot away and its haunting, plaintive wail added to the confusion and din. Eight minutes after the first bomb struck, the *Dorsetshire*'s bow rose high above the sea and within seconds she slid beneath the waves, a victim of seventeen well-aimed bombs.

Simultaneously, much the same fate befell the *Cornwall* when Japanese dive-bombers struck at 1.40pm with the first bomb striking her port side, astern. She swung evasively to starboard as gun crews blazed away, but several were wiped out. It is one of my lasting childhood memories that my dad, Charlie Clancy, a Stoker PO on the *Cornwall* often told us that because he was deep down in the bowels of the ship, working the boilers, he and his shipmates were unaware they were being attacked. When told about it their first reaction was, 'Well if anything happens, at least the *Dorsetshire* is close by to help us'. Imagine their horror when told, 'There's not much she can do. She went down five minutes ago.'

First Lieut. Geoffrey Grove later described his recollections of the attack. "We watched the planes like hawks, and as the bombs showered down, we flung ourselves down on our faces. If the hit was close by, you were bounced like a ball. We had three hits almost directly under

HMS Cornwall sinking, as seen by the Japanese pilots.

us and for one of them I was standing up and was enveloped in a great sheet of flame. I thought it was the end of me but my clothing saved me and I was unhurt. We took something like fifteen hits in about seven minutes and the poor old girl took on a bigger list than ever and started to settle. When I could do no more up top, I went below to help put out the fires and throw red-hot ammunition into the sea. We got all the fires out quite easily. By this time the ship was obviously sinking and some of the men were launching the floats." In not wishing to over-glamorise the situation Grove added that there were some very nasty sights to be seen that day which were far too harrowing to describe. Grove then tells how having got the wounded over the side, he joined them, swam clear of the sinking ship and turned around to witness her final moments. *Cornwall* sank bows first, then her stern rose up high in the air and as she slid down, one propeller was still slowly revolving.

With both cruisers now sinking, the Japanese aircraft formed up into squadrons and flew past in perfect formation. To the relief of the survivors, they flew away. Most expected to be strafed in the water. Survivors later recalled counting the enemy aircraft and said there were 27 dive-bombers and one seaplane but Captain Manwaring of the *Cornwall* was of the opinion the figure was nearer 36 or more; Captain Agar of the *Dorsetshire* suggested it was closer to 50, possibly more. In the heat of battle and its aftermath no one can be sure. The attack on both ships had taken just nineteen minutes. The first dive-bombers had been sighted, already in a dive at 1346hrs and by 1405hrs both ships had vanished beneath the waves. In the attack Egusa's dive-bombers established an all-time record in bombing accuracy with every bomb either hitting its target or scoring a damaging near miss. The explosions came so quickly that many pilots could not see whether they had actually released their bomb load or not. It was only after they had completed the attack and formed up into formation the pilots could check each other's bomb racks to ensure they were not still armed.

In an official report on the loss of the *Cornwall*, written later by Commander J. Fair, he concluded that whilst the ship took numerous well-directed hits, the cause of the sinking in such a short time was probably due to the underwater damage caused by the near misses. It was thought this similarly applied to the *Dorsetshire*. The effect of these near misses was to lift the ship bodily by their force, causing her to twist heavily from stem to stern. It brought down the radio aerials and nearly shook the mast down. Commander Fair recorded that the enemy's bombing had been very accurate with only two real misses having been seen. These were probably due to the attacking aircraft having been hit before releasing their bombs because it is doubtful whether it was sufficiently accurate to allow near misses being deliberately achieved by aircraft fitted with special bombs useful only for this purpose.

These 'special bombs' referred to in the *Cornwall*'s battle report were at first thought to be a depth-charge with a pointed nose cone and small vanes because when it landed in the water, after a brief pause there was a tremendous explosion which caused major under-water damage. Admiral Somerville's view was that although a new method of attack might have been devised, it is more likely that the bombs were in fact, light cased high explosive devices with a short delay fuse which either exploded under water or when they came into contact with the under-water part of the ship. Taking all the evidence into consideration, the Admiralty considered this to be the most likely explanation.

Commander Fair commented that it was noticeable how after dropping their bombs, the Japanese pilots made no effort to regain altitude for a second attack. Instead, they appeared to be offering themselves as targets for the anti-aircraft guns, thus drawing away fire on the following aircraft. From this it was deduced that each aircraft carried only one bomb apiece and that the attack on the *Cornwall* ceased before she sank as all bombs had been expended.

The attack left over a thousand men in two groups in the water some 400 miles from land. As they prepared for nightfall, Captain Agar reassured the men they would have to stay together and stick it out whatever happened. He was certain help would soon come. In a true, stoic British fashion he announced, "The British Navy never leaves its comrades in the lurch". There were many survivors of the "Forlorn Battle of the Java Seas" who might have told him differently, but Agar's confidence was fortunately not misplaced on this occasion.

On the afternoon of the 5th, two hours after the sinking of the two cruisers, a Swordfish spotted the survivors and a destroyer was sent to pick them up but was recalled when it was thought the Japanese were approaching the area. They were in fact some 100 miles to the north, steering south-west. The survivors were heartened at being located but bitterly disappointed when no one arrived to pick them up. By mid-day on the 6th their rescue became Somerville's main concern.

There had been many deaths on both ships, mainly through injuries received in the bombing attack. The bodies were kept within the group to deter the sharks and barracudas of which several were seen but it has been suggested the fuel oil in the water also played a big part in keeping them away. I can recall, when I was a small boy I often asked my dad how he had kept the sharks away and his stock answer would always be, 'We put our heads under the water and made the sound of a swordfish'. I never did find out what that sounded like!

It was important to maintain a high morale but of greater importance was the care of the wounded. Three of the four surgeons from the *Dorsetshire* were casualties themselves, leaving Surgeon Lieut. A.H.F. Wood to attend to the wounded by himself. After establishing a sick bay of sorts in a whaler where he could attend the wounded, Surgeon Lieut. Wood worked tirelessly for 36 hours; many owed their lives to him. *Cornwall's* wounded were gradually marshalled together in the motor boat where they were treated by Surgeon Lieut. Commander H.G. Rees, RNVR, and Surgeon Lieut. P.W. Isaac, RNVR. These two officers worked ceaselessly without rest or food during the whole time they were in the motor boat. It was only when everyone was aboard the rescue ship, the *Enterprise* they and Surgeon Lieut. McEldowney, RNVR, who had been on an outlying float, went straight to the Sick Bay and carried on treating the wounded for a further twenty four hours with only brief breaks for food and sleep.

Throughout that long night, although out of sight, the two groups of survivors occasionally heard each other enjoying a sing-along. The hours passed unbelievably slowly but as dawn broke, the survivors were hopeful that rescue would come soon. Suddenly, across the calm sea came the shrill sound of the bosun's pipe calling *Dorsetshire's* ship's company to breakfast. Everyone laughed enormously. Breakfast? According to one survivor it consisted of salvaged oranges and canteen dripping. The men of the *Cornwall* fared little better. They had a tiny piece of corned beef and tinned apricots, punctured first so that everyone could have a swig of the juice. This proved to be most fortuitous as seawater and oil had contaminated the drinking water in the barricoes. Apricots were thought to be ideal emergency rations as due to their size there are more pieces of this fruit in a tin than any other, so each tin was divided between ten men. However, it was not easy to divide the apricot segments, as my dad often told me. The officer in charge of his boat would take a segment out of the tin, and with his fingers, break it in half, a piece for him and a piece for the next man. Given the soft, wet texture of the fruit, the division was usually two-thirds to one-third – with no prizes for guessing who got the largest share! As well as this, each boat carried emergency rations of water, ship's biscuits and tinned milk.

Throughout the day the survivors continually scanned the horizon for signs of the rescue ships until finally at about 5pm, after twenty-six hours in the water, an aircraft flew overhead signalling "Hold on. Help coming." With darkness fast approaching, at around 6pm the cruiser *Enterprise* and the destroyers *Paladin* and *Panther* arrived to pick up the exhausted survivors. An air search was also provided to assist and a fighter escort covered the rescue operation.

Why had it taken the rescue ships so long to reach the survivors? Their position was known to the fleet and given that the planned rendezvous was scheduled for Sunday afternoon at 5pm, this should have been only four hours away from the site of the sinking. As it turned out, the rescue ships took twenty-four, twelve of which were in daylight. It seems likely there was an order from Somerville telling them to hold back until Japanese movements were more clearly understood.

The sinking of these two cruisers was a major tragedy for the British but equally a brilliant display of the effectiveness of the Japanese carrier-borne aircraft. The attack on the two ships had been so sudden and its consequences so quick that news of it did not reach the C-in-C for some while. He assumed that the absence of communications from both ships was simply the result of strict radio silence being kept. It was not until the next day that it was suspected disaster had befallen both ships.

In his book, *Destroyer Man*, Rear Admiral Pugsley, at the time Captain of the *Paladin*, described what he saw at the scene of the sinking. The Captains of the three ships had been sent to investigate two positions about 12 miles apart from which the last enemy report had been received. The first thing to catch Captain Pugsley's eye was a mast with its tip high out of the water and from

Survivors being taken aboard the *Paladin*.

where a thick, black stream of oil was stretching away to the leeward. Without knowing exactly what it was they were investigating, and from the amount of oil floating on the surface, it was thought a tanker had been sunk. As the *Paladin* steamed alongside the oil slick the ship's crew could see that it was a confused mass of one or two small boats, some floats and hundreds of men struggling to keep afloat in the thick, glutinous mass of oil. It was later thought that the mass of oil had deterred attacks by sharks. This was all that remained of the *Dorsetshire*. A similar scene must have greeted the crews of the *Panther* and the *Enterprise* as they headed towards what remained of the *Cornwall*.

The survivors from the *Dorsetshire* were divided between the *Paladin* and the *Panther* whilst most of the *Cornwall's* survivors were taken aboard the *Enterprise*. The men were taken to Addu Atoll where a supply ship had been converted to a temporary hospital ship. The Eastern Fleet had just arrived there and for most of the men it was the first time they had seen the Atoll. Their initial impression was that it was all very primitive, but it worked. Out of a total complement of 1,546 officers and men in the two cruisers, 1,122 survived. Captain Agar of the *Dorsetshire* later described this as '… a miracle, but in reality it was the spirit of courage and faith that did it.'

Later, Lieut-Commander Egusa who had led the attack was asked how his aircraft had managed to sink the British cruisers so quickly. He said somewhat arrogantly, it had been much simpler than bombing the *Settsu*, Japan's old target practice battleship. In a short space of time the Japanese naval airmen had shown that their dive-bombers could be just as effective against ships at sea as the land-based, high-level and torpedo-bombers of the Saigon-based Air Corps that had sunk the *Prince of Wales* and the *Repulse*. Japan had to be recognized as masters of the air. Our main weapon with which to fight back was our Eastern Fleet but if surface vessels could not immediately be brought into action, we had the carriers *Formidable* and *Indomitable* which each had a squadron of Swordfish and Albacore aircraft. They were no match against the superior Japanese Zeros that would have hopelessly outnumbered them, of course and it is difficult to see what effect these slow, old biplanes would have had.

We now know that in order to bring the enemy ships within the Swordfish's limited range our carriers would have to steam in for a further fifty or sixty miles, or at least within the perimeter of the Japanese dive bombers' effective range before our own aircraft could be launched. Night operations from carriers then, as now, presented enormous difficulties and risks, but it was an option that Somerville had considered.

Frustratingly there was little Somerville could do to avenge the loss of the *Cornwall* and the *Dorsetshire*. He was not willing to take his battleships with their low endurance capability too far eastwards and away from their base. He hoped his search planes might locate the enemy at night using their radar so that he could attack at night, but this plan failed and neither fleet succeeded in finding the other. The most dangerous moment was now at hand. The two fleets were only 180 miles apart with both Admirals unaware of each other's position and with just four hours of daylight left.

With no information of the enemy's movements having been received for more than 24 hours and nothing having happened to alter the possibility of them being in the vicinity of Addu Atoll, either to attack it by air on 6th April or to await the return of the Eastern Fleet, Somerville decided to set an easterly course to secure a position from which he could successfully launch an attack on the Japanese should they go to Addu Atoll. Finally Somerville received a signal from Sir Geoffrey Layton, Commander-in-Chief, Ceylon, informing him that there was a strong Japanese force somewhere between Addu Atoll and Colombo. Somerville decided therefore, not to approach Addu Atoll until sometime after daybreak on 7th April. Instead, he ordered an extensive air search of the north-east sector and four Albacores of No. 827 Squadron took off from the *Indomitable* at 1400 hrs on diverging courses for 200 miles. In view of the Albacore's low speed and vulnerability, it might have been more prudent to have used Fulmars as search planes, but no doubt Somerville wanted to conserve what few fighters he had.

One pilot on this patrol was Sub-Lt. R.D. Smith was also looking-out for the two cruisers, not knowing by now they had been sunk, but he returned to report he had not seen either the cruisers or the Japanese fleet.

A point to consider at this juncture is, if Nagumo was keen to engage the Eastern Fleet, where did he think the two cruisers were heading for at such high speed if not to join their fleet? Had he extended his air search ahead of them to the south, he would undoubtedly have sighted Somerville's Force A and been in an ideal position from which to launch an overwhelming attack. This was, afterall, Nagumo's prime reason for being in the Indian Ocean. Instead, Nagumo altered course to a south-easterly direction with his main force, leaving two carriers and their escorts behind to await the return of the strike force of Vals. They were all recovered by 1600 hrs and the ships turned south-easterly to rejoin the main force. The reason for Nagumo changing course was probably part of a pre-arranged plan to rendezvous with an oil tanker and refuel his ships before moving into position for the attack on Trincomalee. It is doubtful whether he was now seriously looking for the Eastern Fleet.

Meanwhile, the pilot of another of the four Albacores, Sub-Lt. Streathfield, passed over the wreckage from the two cruisers at 1500 hrs and radioed a report on its position. Fifteen minutes later he spotted the main Japanese force but was shot down before he had time to send in a sighting report. Had he been able to do so it might have given Somerville the vital information that the enemy was retiring to the south-east, thus giving Somerville an opportunity to carry out his plan for a night torpedo attack.

Another Albacore pilot to spot the enemy fleet was Sub-Lt. Grant-Sturgis who was on the most westerly leg of the search area. He managed to radio a sighting report before being attacked by a Zero. Grant-Sturgis dropped down to sea level and managed to escape from the Zero which because of this was forced to break off the attack.

At 11am on 8th April the Eastern Fleet returned to Addu Atoll where it immediately began refuelling. Somerville called a meeting with his

Flag- and Commanding Officers to discuss the situation and explain his intentions. The experiences of the last few days had left no doubts in Somerville's mind as to the undesirability of further operations in the waters around Ceylon for the time being at least. He sent a report to this effect to the Admiralty in which he told their Lordships how the Japanese appeared to have complete control of the Bay of Bengal and could at any time take command of the waters to the south and south-west of Ceylon. No one in the fleet had any doubt by this time that they were up against a most powerful and dangerous concentration of the enemy.

Somerville believed that the Allied naval and land-based aircraft at our disposal were woefully inadequate to offer sustained opposition to the far superior Japanese forces. He recognized that his ships were slow, outgunned and of short endurance, so they were only a liability, whilst the availability of carrier-borne air defences would be of little effect against repeated attacks on the scale used against the *Dorsetshire* and the *Cornwall*. There was little security against air or surface attacks at the Ceylon naval bases and none at all at Addu Atoll. For these reasons Somerville decided to send his Force B, the older, slower and out-gunned ships, *Ramillies, Resolution, Royal Sovereign*, and *Revenge*, to the naval base at Kilindini near Mombasa where it could offer effective protection to the Middle East and Persian Gulf line of communications and at the same time, undergo some collective training. This was an order endorsed by Churchill himself who said "On one point we were all agreed, the Rs should get out of danger at the earliest moment. When I put this to the First Sea Lord there was no need for argument. Orders were sent accordingly". Admiral Willis prepared for their departure westwards with an escort of destroyers and with them went the survivors of the *Dorsetshire* and the *Cornwall*. They departed from Addu Atoll on 9th April.

At the same time Force A, the faster and better-equipped element of the fleet, set sail for Bombay from where it would continue to operate in the Indian Ocean to deter the Japanese from attacking lines of communication there with light forces but for the immediate future would avoid Ceylon. Only a few auxiliaries and supply ships were to remain at Addu Atoll. Bombay was far from being ideal as a base but it was nearer than Mombasa if a presence in the Indian Ocean was to be maintained. Upon receipt of Somerville's report and having been informed of the facts of the Japanese successes, the Admiralty ordered the Eastern Fleet not to return to the Ceylon harbours. They had decided, for the time being at least, to concede the eastern part of the Indian Ocean to the Japanese.

Whilst en route to Bombay Somerville decided to make a brief visit to Colombo to discuss the current situation with Admiral Layton but it was too late. The curtain had already been raised on the final episode in this drama, a surprise attack on Trincomalee in which the Eastern Fleet was to play no part and which instead, forced it to proceed post haste to the safety of Bombay. Throughout the voyage to Bombay a close watch was kept for the Japanese fleet, but where were they? It was unlikely we'd seen the last of them. This was a possibility no one seems to have considered. Most were still of the opinion of the likelihood of an invasion of either Ceylon or southern India. The Japanese were in fact bombarding the east coast of India and scores of freighters in the Bay of Bengal had been attacked and sunk. But Japan's successes that day were not yet over.

The morning had started badly for Admiral Somerville with several disturbing distress signals being received from six merchant ships that formed a loose, straggling convoy that was hugging the coastline on a southerly course in the area of Vizagapatam. None of these vessels survived the day. They were the *Autolycus*, the *Indora*, the *Malda*, the *Exmoor*, the *Silksworth* and the *Shinkuang*.

During the afternoon two aircraft from the *Ryujo*, the carrier in Vice-Admiral Ozawa's Malaya Force had found another target southeast of Vizagapatam, the merchant ship *Dardanus* that was still following the coastal route southwards. Bombs struck her engine room and she was brought to an abrupt halt. As the ship's boats got away, a second attack took place scoring more direct hits. Once the aircraft had left, Captain English and some of his crew returned to the ship, plugged some of the holes and got the pumps working. The British India Company steamer *Gandara* arrived on the scene and took the stricken *Dardanus* under tow, heading for Madras. As night fell, the two ships were making steady headway and the prospect of salvaging the *Dardanus* was looking good. Unfortunately the two vessels were in a recognized sea-lane which the Japanese had under close surveillance.

Early the following morning a Japanese flying boat flew overhead. It had taken off at dawn from the Andaman Islands where there was an anchorage at Port Blair. It was standard Japanese practice for her reconnaissance aircraft to carry a small bomb load, and the *Gandara* and the *Dardanus* were easy targets. They both carried limited armament which they used against the flying boat but the pilot was not deterred. With its bomb load gone and both ships still afloat and under way, he called for a surface vessel to complete the job. Three cruisers answered the call at high speed, firing relentlessly at the two merchantmen but still they miraculously stayed afloat. The *Gandara* was forced to slip her tow rope as a fourth ship, a light cruiser, approached to join the fray and after blasting the two ships with shellfire, they were finally sunk with torpedoes. The *Dardanus'* boats reached the shore on the 7th and amazingly after their ordeal none of her crew was missing. The *Gandara* however, did lose a few men.

A second Japanese spotter plane, possibly a seaplane, had taken off from one of the cruisers and began to patrol an area 150 miles north of the flying boat's search area. It too found a suitable target, the *Autolycus*, still on its way south from Calcutta. Upon leaving port her skipper, Captain Neville had been told by a naval control service officer that there was a large fleet in the vicinity. He did not make it clear whether it was hostile or not; Captain Neville assumed it to be friendly. Spotters on the *Autolycus* identified the incoming seaplane as hostile and opened fire. Captain Neville was relieved to see warships coming over the horizon towards him but that soon turned to dismay as he realized they were about to open fire. The shells fell steadily and accurately on the ship, forcing her crew to abandon her. Most of the crew managed to make landfall at Orissa but sixteen lives were lost.

Throughout that week there were many such incidents of which the world heard little. On the east coast the surface raiders' toll was 23 ships, totalling 112,000 tons. Submarines, mainly deployed on the west coast, added a further five to bring the total tonnage to 144,000. The sinking of these ships was unexpected and the merchant seamen were angry that no protection was offered either by sea or in the air.

With all this activity taking place off the coast of India, coupled with the news of the attack on Colombo having been released, many believed that a similar raid on Madras was bound to follow. As boatloads of survivors from the stricken merchant ships were spotted all along the coast, it fuelled speculation of an imminent Japanese invasion. This was the belief of the Governor of Madras Sir Arthur Hope who issued a general warning of such an invasion, resulting in Government departments beginning a planned evacuation, and even the troops put into effect their planned immobilizing operations in the port and started to dismantle the rail tracks. Tension quickly spread throughout southern India. An air-raid warning was sounded on 6th April and an exodus of the population began. It is still not clear why the warning was given or on whose instructions because there were no aircraft approaching either the city or the harbour at the time. A few bombs were dropped on Cocinada and Vizagapatam but they caused little damage. Whereas the attack on Colombo had an adverse effect on Madras, the rest of the world saw the result as a most welcome surprise. The raid was described as 'A large-scale air attack on Colombo, with indifferent results and heavy losses inflicted on the enemy.' Furthermore, it was implied that this was an invasion force – which the authorities had for some time believed to be so – but as they had failed to gain air superiority, the enemy had withdrawn. As a matter of policy news of the loss of the warships was never reported at the time. It would have been far too useful to the enemy. Merchant ship losses were not mentioned at all.

When news like this was released to the media it was described as a communiqué. A great deal of skill and tact went into writing them, and both sides exercised their ingenuity to its limits. Whilst generally seen by the public as good news of our successes, the Chiefs of Staff Committee in London were under no illusions as to how serious the situation really was. Any reassurances the news might have conveyed was tempered by the general apprehension in Madras, as elsewhere, that there was more to come.

In retrospect, the British paid dearly for underestimating Japanese capabilities. After Pearl Harbour, the loss of *HMS Repulse* and *HMS Prince of Wales*, and the fall of Singapore greater caution might have been expected. It is easy to apportion blame afterwards, but it did seem unwise to send *Dorsetshire* back to Colombo for a second time to finish her refit with a huge Japanese fleet threatening. This was Somerville's decision, but we do not know what other viable choices he had. Certainly, South Africa was a safer place for a refit, but it was also so far away that *Dorsetshire* would not have been able to get back in time to assist in any action and Somerville needed every ship he had under his command. It leads to questions such as, was Bombay too crowded; and did the ship really need the refit at this critical juncture? It must be remembered that Somerville had to choose his time for battle carefully. If he was caught in the open, he would surely lose to the larger Japanese fleet with all its dive bombers and torpedo bombers. He had divided his fleet into a fast part and a slow part, holding the latter in reserve. *Dorsetshire* had been assigned to the fast division where speed was essential for a fast night attack, in and out before aircraft could reach them, hence Somerville's insistence on a refit to increase her speed.

The rendezvous point for the cruisers with the main British fleet was set too far east, too close to the Japanese. *Dorsetshire* should have steamed due west at dawn when it was learned how close the Japanese were but had no reason to believe Somerville would not show up at the rendezvous point, expecting the help of two cruisers for a night attack on the Japanese aircraft carriers. He knew he was taking a great risk.

But what of Somerville's failure to find the Japanese fleet where they were expected to be? It was not until after the end of the war that the mystery of where the Japanese were came to light. Aerial reconnaissance showed that they had turned tail and had started to head for the East Indies but not before they had carried out one more attack on Ceylon as planned. This time the target was to be Trincomalee. The Japanese High Command were concerned at the possibility of their Task Force in the Indian Ocean being cut off from the remainder of their naval forces in the South China Seas as the result of increasing American naval activity in the South Pacific, and had ordered a retreat. It was a missed opportunity for the Japanese because they could have easily advanced into East Africa and beyond, given the light level of resistance the British could offer. Had they seized the opportunity it could have completely changed the course of the war.

As Somerville was steaming north to Bombay, his adversary, Nagumo, was heading eastwards, back to Singapore where his fleet was needed to take part in operations aimed at the capture of Port Moresby as a part of the Japanese southward drive towards Australia. The tide of Japanese expansion had reached its zenith, and following the Battle of the Coral Sea in May and the Battle of Midway in June, it marked the end of Japanese naval air power's domination of the Pacific. The Imperial Japanese Navy could never again threaten the British in the Indian Ocean.

CHAPTER 6

Survivors' Stories

Here is a selection of accounts of what it was like to 'Abandon Ship', written by survivors, principally of the *Dorsetshire* and the *Cornwall*, mainly because I was unable to find any similar accounts for survivors from the other ships sunk at this time.

Geoffrey Kitchen

Geoff was a Royal Marine serving aboard *HMS Dorsetshire* and during action stations was a part of the gun crew manning a twin four-inch HA/LA gun. He had been aboard the ship for two years and described it as a happy ship. Just two months earlier he had celebrated his 19th birthday. On the day of the attack the ship's company had been at action stations since at least 8am. The battle ensign was fluttering aloft and all gun crews were closed-up. Everyone on deck kept glancing skywards, ready for the attack they knew was coming. The heat from the tropical sun was almost overpowering especially on those parts of the ship that escaped from the breeze as the ship sped along at 28 knots. It was too hot to move around much and the lookouts were relieved every quarter of an hour.

At 11.30am an aircraft was seen low on the horizon, disappearing from view every few minutes. *Dorsetshire's* Commander and Executive Officer, Commander Byas, a Fleet Air Arm pilot, identified it as being Japanese. Shortly after 1pm confused streaks were seen on the radar screen. The warning to stand by was given and the gun crews made ready. Guns were trained fore and aft as far as their mountings allowed. Normally the fire from the four-inch guns would be controlled by a Director to give the most concentrated form of fire. On this occasion however, the order came for the gun crew to go into local control, i.e. guns to fire on targets of their own choice.

Suddenly dive-bombers swooped in without any warning from out of the sun in waves of three. Geoff remembers seeing the *Cornwall* under attack, receiving a direct hit aft within seconds. He said he was aware of the noise of the planes' engines as they swooped down. They didn't sound very powerful, probably because the pilots decreased speed as they levelled out at just above mast height to launch their bombs. A shadow passed over his gun deck temporarily blotting out the sunlight; there was a blast of hot air and grey ash from the funnels showered everywhere. Geoff was flung against the steel plating surrounding the gun mounting. The Walrus seaplane and its catapult were hit. There was a blinding flash as the Fleet Air Arm's workshop containing high-octane aviation fuel exploded into an inferno. The captain of the gun yelled to the crew to reload, a difficult manoeuvre in the now chaotic conditions. The ship had slewed around and was heeling over. The ammunition lockers had fallen and several live shells were rolling around the deck. As Geoff struggled to his feet a second bomb struck the starboard side of the after funnel where there was another Royal Marines gun crew within twelve feet of where the bomb struck. The after funnel started to lean over across his gun deck on the port side.

The next bomb fell just forward of Geoff's position but by this time he was unable to see clearly as a steel splinter had cut a deep furrow across his skull and blood was pouring over his eyes. The noise of the battle was deafening. Bomb after bomb rained down, each hitting their target with uncanny accuracy. *Dorsetshire* was listing to port, her steering gear jammed and she was starting to settle by the stern; she was doomed. A shout came from the wrecked bridge to abandon ship and Geoff started to inflate his lifebelt but it had been ripped and was of no use. He was not unduly worried by this as he was a strong swimmer. After helping several injured shipmates over the side, Geoff joined them in the water where at last he could wash the blood from his injury out of his eyes. After the turmoil of the attack the sea seemed quite peaceful. As he struck out to join other survivors swimming some distance away, a Petty Officer called out, "She's going lads. Give her a cheer." The bows slipped beneath the waves and Geoff felt himself being pulled under. He swam frantically away from the deadly undertow.

He recalls there was a dreadful smell of diesel oil with huge blobs of the stuff floating on the surface, covering all the swimmers. Men were retching and choking everywhere. There was no panic. The men were quietly talking to each other as they formed up into small groups, clinging to any available wreckage they could find, and calling out for news of their shipmates.

The only boats to get away as the ship sank were two whalers and a skiff that were used to put the injured into. A few small Denton life rafts had also floated off. From time to time more wreckage surfaced as the ship started to break up thousands of feet beneath the waves. One particular lifesaver that came up was a section of the ship's main mast. Unlike many of the other County Class cruisers, *Dorsetshire* still had her original wooden mast. Everyone was optimistic they would be rescued by nightfall, after all they were little more than 90 miles from their planned rendezvous point with the rest of the fleet. Another useful item that surfaced was a 20lb tin of dripping and some oranges, which were divided equally between the two whalers and given to the injured. The dripping was used to rub on their bodies to keep out the cold at night and as protection against the hot sun by day. Amongst the wreckage, someone spotted a tiny kitten clinging to a piece of wood. The survivors passed it hand over hand until it reached the comparative safety of a whaler where the Chief Buffer put it inside his singlet to keep warm.

Despite night falling, spirits did not diminish. Although the night air was cold, the sea stayed warm. It was difficult trying to keep awake and if a man's head started to droop, those nearest to him would prod him awake. As the injured in the whalers died some of those in the water took their place, but the dead sailors were kept in the boats for fear of their bodies attracting sharks. Geoff was offered a place and recalled it was particularly unpleasant in the whaler with the dead and severely injured. He soon gave up his place and got back into the water, finding a position holding on to the mast.

Throughout that long, cold night morale never faltered and as the sun started to rise, the ever-resourceful sailors and Marines made hats out their shorts, singlets and odd scraps of canvas to protect themselves from the fierce tropical sun. By noon spirits had started to flag as the men realized that if the fleet had located the Japanese, every ship and aircraft would be needed for the action. None could be spared for search and rescue. To raise their morale the Captain ordered another small ration of milk and water be distributed to all. It was now 24 hours since the ship had gone down and unbeknown to the survivors, their ordeal was nearly over. At 4pm Lieut-Commander Durant spotted an aircraft which he identified as being "one of ours". Everyone waved jubilantly as it got nearer and up went the shout, "Stringbag". It was a Fleet Air Arm Fairey Swordfish which flashed the reassuring message, "Help coming. Hold on." There was just two hours of daylight left and many feared the fading light would thwart the rescue. The time passed slowly, then at 6.30pm the light cruiser *HMS Enterprise* appeared, accompanied by the destroyers *Paladin* and *Panther*. *Enterprise* and *Panther* headed for the *Cornwall's* survivors who were quite close by but who could not be seen due to the waves by the survivors of the *Dorsetshire*, whilst the *Paladin*, a Royal Australian Navy vessel came to the aid of the *Dorsetshire* survivors.

Everyone scrambled aboard the rescue ship where they were offered food and drink. The tiny bathrooms on board could not accommodate everyone but it didn't matter as the men washed off as much fuel oil as they could on deck. Everyone was just grateful to be alive after their ordeal. Accommodation was limited on the destroyer and the men slept wherever they could find a space. Geoff was given a blanket and remembers wrapping himself in it before curling up in a Carley float on top of a torpedo tube and getting a good night's sleep. The rescue ships then headed for Addu Atoll, our secret base in the Maldives where although there was no hospital to receive the wounded, a storeship was hastily converted and used until the hospital ship *Vita* could get there from Ceylon.

Plans were made for the walking and lightly wounded to remain ashore at Addu Atoll until they could be evacuated to East Africa. All other survivors from both the *Cornwall* and the *Dorsetshire* would be distributed between the four R-Class battleships to continue with the war at sea.

Walter Fudge

Walter also served aboard the *Dorsetshire* but as a sailor, and like Geoff Kitchen, he too had been aboard in 1941 when the ship had attacked the German battleship *Bismarck*. Walter recalls how after the Japanese attack, two of his shipmates went below to their mess, refusing to leave the ship. They said they were non-swimmers and would not stand a chance once in the sea. He said similarly Captain Agar had intended going down with his ship but was bundled unceremoniously over the side by someone named Cassier who said he'd not allow it.

Whilst many records of the attack say the Japanese did not strafe the seamen in the water, Walter refutes this and says he later found a machine gun bullet lodged just under the skin of his ankle, its velocity probably having been slowed down as it hit the water. Similarly many deny that sharks attacked the swimmers but Walter says he knows of at least one incident. After over thirty hours in the water, Walter still remembers the welcoming site of the *Paladin* coming to the rescue, on board which he enjoyed at least a dozen cups of tea then slept on deck all the way to Mombasa for a week's leave before joining the battleship *Valiant*.

Charlie Clancy

Like many of those who came home from the war, seemingly unscathed, my father spoke very little about this incident in which he could well have perished. Clinging to a small piece of wreckage some three feet square and eating only a tiny piece of apricot, his first "meal" in more than 24 hours, is one of the lasting memories Charlie Clancy has after leaving the comparative safety of *HMS Cornwall*. And of course, the fear of being unprotected in shark-infested waters.

At the time of the attack Charlie, a Stoker PO, was on duty in the engine room and when the order came to abandon ship, he had to struggle up through the bowels of the doomed ship in the gloom with other sailors. He said, not knowing what was happening outside we were all confident the *Dorsetshire* would come to our aid but then someone broke the news that she had also been attacked and was sinking fast. On deck it sounded like hailstones were landing as the Japanese aircraft raked the vessel from stem to stern with machine gun fire. The survivors then had to spend the next 28 hours in water thick with fuel oil and they could see for themselves that any hopes of their sister ship *Dorsetshire* coming to their aid were dashed. She had sunk minutes previously.

Having struck out away from the sinking ship and its deadly undertow, Charlie found himself in a patch of crystal clear water. He looked down and saw a shark beneath him. It appeared to be getting fatter and smaller, and Charlie knew it was coming up to the surface. The resourceful sailors soon discovered however that by slapping their hands up and down on the water's surface the noise seemed to deter the sharks and they swam away. In all their time in the water there was not one single shark attack. But the intense fear each man felt remained with them forever.

Bob Crick

When the first bomb fell on the *Cornwall* Bob Crick, a former Chief Engine Room Artificer was laying up on deck with some shipmates getting a breath of fresh air. His first indication that the ship was under attack was when he heard a terrific "whoosh" and he was soaked by a huge waterspout. Bob was 30 at the time and had been on the *Cornwall* for three years. One of his lasting memories is at the time of their rescue, whichever way you looked all you could see were oil-covered sailors clambering into lifeboats. Many of those who survived still bear the scars to this day and at a Reunion Dinner held in 1982 Bob was shown the burnt, oil-stained legs of another survivor.

Bob was quick to pay tribute to the families who had been left behind at home, not knowing what was happening to their loved ones. They suffered their own trials and tribulations. In Bob's case, he said good-bye to his wife Gladys in 1939 and apart from a short weekend break in Liverpool, didn't see her again until 1942 when he came home as a survivor.

Teddie Drew

Lieutenant (E) E.A. Drew served on the *Cornwall* for sixteen months prior to her sinking. During the Forenoon Watch, Teddie had been at his action station i/c Forward Damage Control Party. Just before noon he was relieved to get some food and then sent to relieve Mike Edgar in the After Engine Room. The first those in the engine room knew of the attack was a terrific bang, the ship shuddering and clouds of dust billowing from the supply ventilation fans. There were several more explosions and the After Engine Room lost main steam. The lights went out and there was pitch darkness. A bomb exploded at the after end of the Engine Room with dense smoke and flames visible against the deckhead.

Teddie shouted to the lads to get out and even in the pitch-black darkness everyone knew where the sole exit ladder was. Just as he was leaving, being the last man out, Teddie heard a scream from the after end. He went towards it but it stopped. He remembers thinking to himself, "My lot's up. It's all over. I won't get out of here." and just as he felt ready to sit down and wait for the end, he realized he had a wife and child and must make the effort to get out. Somehow he got back to the ladder and started to climb. His way was blocked by smoke and flames but he pushed on and apart from burns to his hands and legs, soon found himself on the main deck with only one other companionway to negotiate to reach the upper deck. By this time the ship had developed a severe list to port, which made moving across the deck extremely difficult. Teddie was all in; he was in a state of shock and badly injured.

The ship was still under attack and could not fight back. She was a sitting duck. Someone helped Teddie to the upper deck on the port side where the sea was by now lapping the deck. As he lay there, preparing to go over the side the minute the order was given, he heard Lieut (E) 'Archie' Archbold suddenly say, "God, I've left 50 quid in my cabin", and below he went to get it despite efforts to stop him. He returned in time to hear the skipper order 'abandon ship'.

Once in the water, Teddie was quickly covered in fuel oil and could hardly open his eyes. He had to stretch his head back and peer along his cheeks to see what was happening. Suddenly he realized he did not have a lifebelt; it was an offence to be at sea on duty without wearing one. He started to swim away from the sinking ship but found he was slowly being drawn back. He realized the starboard outer propeller was still rotating, with the shaft at water level. He was in big trouble and there was little Teddie could do about it. Suddenly the ship lurched over to port, the propeller came out of the water and Teddie shot by beneath it.

He came across Sub-Lieut. Dougall, a Royal Canadian Navy Volunteer Reserve, who was on the *Cornwall* for training. He had a lifebelt and seeing that Teddie did not, took one from a dead sailor and helped Teddie put it on. Teddie is also adamant that the survivors were strafed in the water despite official records suggesting otherwise.

From the sea, Teddie watched the *Cornwall* falling apart. The Walrus seaplane floated off its catapult but was sunk by the ship's wireless aerials falling across her wings. The seaman in the lookout barrel at the top of the foremast had to remain there throughout the action until he was able to jump into the sea from a height of eight feet as the ship listed over to port. One of the ship's motorboats floated off intact and became the senior boat amongst the Carley floats.

By now Teddie was about half-a-mile astern of the sinking ship, alone and aware of the dead bodies, large fish and wreckage all around him. He found a mess deck tabletop measuring 3 ft by 10 ft which although not possible to get on to, he was able to hold on to it and rest. The ship's Physical Training Petty Officer swam by heading for the motorboat and suggested Teddie accompanied him. He said he'd follow as he was not such a strong swimmer. No sooner had he left his tabletop however he trod on a large fish; he was soon back with his tabletop. Teddie reasoned he had to reach the motorboat by nightfall otherwise he'd be alone all night, so he summoned up the courage and headed for the motorboat which he reached just as darkness started to fall. Once in the motorboat, Commander Fair put Teddie in charge of a Carley float containing 20 ratings. The floats were all lashed around the motorboat to keep them together.

The procedure for the following day was much the same as already described by Geoff Kitchen in his account. On a lighter note, 'Archie' Archbold who had earlier returned to his cabin to retrieve his £50, decided to remove his flannel trousers from beneath his boiler suit, a job that stretched ingenuity in the restricted space and below water. It took him the best part of an hour but eventually the trousers were cast adrift. 'Archie' then realized the precious £50 was still in the back pocket of those trousers!

A curious coincidence happened next for Teddie. He and some of the survivors were picked up by the *Enterprise*. He was taken below, cleaned up and put to bed by a Marine in the cabin of Lieut. Baker. Coincidentally, both Lieut. Baker and Teddie had joined the RNVR on the same night in November 1937 and had met each other for the first time since then when both of their ships were in Colombo just a few weeks previously. Of all the ships to rescue Teddie, of all the cabins to be taken to, what a coincidence.

Of all the survivors' stories to have emerged following this attack, this next one is the most graphic as it clearly recalls what it was like during the attack, the time in the water awaiting rescue and the rescue itself.

Francis Anstis, Stoker 1st Class

When the attack took place Francis was in the worse possible place on the *Dorsetshire*, in the boiler room, three decks down and well below the waterline. Only two out of the seven men in the boiler room survived. One of those was Tom Shirley, Stoker PO who explained how the ship suddenly shuddered, the water level gauges fractured hissing out water and steam, and the lights went out. The ship was in virtual darkness, except for the glow from the fires through the ducting. Tom said they were going at top speed at the time, twenty-eight knots, and after the shudder said, "They've started" (attacking us)" and, "That's our eight-inch forward guns firing a broadside". He had experienced target practice on the *Dorsetshire* and when you fire eight-inch twin guns close up, that really shakes you; crockery would tumble off the shelves and break. There was no order to abandon ship, not even from the Chief Stoker, George Whooley, but Tom turned to Francis and said; "Let's go", and the two men went up the starboard ladder. Tom went first and Francis followed tight on his heels, shaking like a leaf. He said, "I followed him into an air lock that was used to restrict the flow of air to the boiler rooms below. The air lock door was open and we went up another deck to where the force fans were. They were stopped and it was mighty hot. We came up level with the main deck that would have been our normal exit, the deck below the upper deck. We looked for our lifebelts that we hung up just inside the normal exit but they were gone and the exit was a ball of fire blowing in gas and smoke. There was no way anyone could get through there. I looked around and thought we were going to burn to death right there."

Tom had been on the ship longer than Francis and knew there was a service ladder, which took them up to a very small exit on the main deck. Francis said, "We came out on the deck amidships and breathed fresh air. Tom went first and I scrambled out behind him but Tom was soon out of sight. The sight that greeted me was horrific, bodies, body parts, blood, screaming men in agonies of pain, a terrible sight, and this unnerved me rather. The ship was listing to starboard and going down by the stern."

"By now the ship was covered (with water) up to amidships, and the bows rose fifty feet into the air with the flooded stern section filling rapidly with water. I looked across to the port side of the ship that was very quiet because everyone was jumping off the starboard side, the lowest part. I went over to the port side to clear my eyes from the sights I had seen. Suddenly I heard the clatter of the fighter planes machine-gunning the port and starboard in groups of three. I looked up and saw a Japanese fighter quite close by. I could see the cockpit, the pilot's face, his goggles, his equipment, and the bullets coming from the machine gun. I straightened myself up against the steel bulkhead only about six feet away from the guardrail. About seven or eight machine gun bullets hit the deck within six inches of my feet. I waited for this plane to clear; everything was happening in seconds."

"I ran forward towards the bows and another plane came in doing the same thing. I sheltered under the 8-inch "A" gun turret on the foc'sle main deck until that and another plane had cleared. I then ran to the guardrail, stripped off my boiler suit and shirt, kicked off my boots and got on the outside of the guardrail. With my hands behind me, I jumped into the water and finished up in a pile of wreckage and thick black oil the state of treacle, which had congealed in the cold sea. I hit the sea pretty hard and without a lifebelt to break the fall I must have gone below the water at least half the distance I had jumped from the deck and came up spluttering oil, frightened to death. I went down again, came up and was sick, bringing up a lot of oil that was in my mouth and throat. I struck out, I wasn't a very good swimmer, and I swam away from the ship, probably fifty or sixty yards until I could swim no more."

According to the Captain who was watching men jumping off towards the very end, he said it was a height of at least fifty feet. He saw someone stripping off his dark blue uniform and kicking his boots off on deck just before the ship sank. He presumed it was the engine room branch and it could have been Francis he was watching, but he couldn't say for sure. He specifically mentioned this story in his report.

Francis continues. "What with the oil taking effect and the frightening state of affairs, I was exhausted and all I could do was to kick out and tread water. I rested a moment and turned round. I saw the bows of the ship sliding gently back into the sea. In less than two or three seconds it had disappeared, and the *Dorsetshire* was on its way to the bottom. I panicked and looked around me. There were groups of men at different places because we had drifted away from the ship. I shouted for help at the top of my voice because I had no lifebelt and if I couldn't tread water any more I knew I was going to drown. I shouted for help twice and someone came over to me; he was a very good swimmer, I don't know who he was but we had a lot of Australians and South Africans on board who were marvellous swimmers. He shouted to me, 'Hold on' and brought me a blown-up lifebelt. He managed to get it on me and said, 'You're OK now. Just rest a minute or two and then get back to the lads'. He swam in front of me and after resting a couple of times, we eventually reached the nearest group of men that were hanging on to a part of the main mast that had floated off or it could have been one of the booms that were used for the motorboats in the harbour."

There were about eighteen or twenty men hanging on to the boom but they made space for me on it. I was absolutely exhausted. The ship had disappeared and there was a lot of noise from other groups of men who were badly wounded and dying. When I jumped into the water I had hit my left groin badly on some wreckage, gashed my foot and scalded my arm on a steam pipe or a jet of steam. I hadn't felt any pain because the salt water seemed to numb it but apart from my wounds, complete shock was now getting hold of me but I felt safe. I was hanging on and we were helping each other, talking and trying to blank out things. There was a shout of sharks being in the area around the main group. I hadn't seen any personally but some of the other survivors had and many of the floating dead bodies had disappeared which we presumed were taken by sharks. We weren't actually attacked because it was thought that the smell of the black oil and the noise had deterred them. We had been told by the skipper to make noise and splash to keep the sharks at bay.

Whilst in the water three Jap fighter planes came low over the survivors, machine gunning. I thought after all I had been through I was about to die with a machine gun bullet in me. I let go of the boom and forced myself under the water hoping this would lessen the force of the bullets, but no one was hit as far as I know and whether they were trying to hit us or scare us, I'm not sure. One of the planes did a victory roll, joined the other two and presumably went back to join their carrier. We were in the water approximately thirty hours from 1.30pm on Easter Sunday. The attack lasted around eight minutes in total; my watch stopped at 1.30pm as I hit the sea because it wasn't waterproof.

We weren't too concerned about hunger because we had just eaten a good dinner before the attack took place; it was the thirst that worried us. The Japanese were very clever in not starting their attack until the sun was high in the sky so it upset our guns' accuracy. I later read a Japanese report that they dived from the sun on purpose. The Japanese reported they dropped thirteen one thousand pound bombs and scored eleven direct hits on the ship. Eventually everyone got into one main group and the badly wounded were put into two boats with the doctors helping people in the greatest pain. After about four hours several Fairey Swordfish aircraft, which were carried on all cruisers, were sent out to look for us. They knew roughly the area where we were. The Swordfish came in right over us signalling with their Aldis lamp "Hang on, help coming". Our signals section was able to pick the message up and this was conveyed to everyone. We were happy; we cheered, watched the horizon and thought it will be no time now before we were found. We were aware that the *Cornwall* had been bombed and sunk nearby so there was another group of men in the vicinity in exactly the same position as us, but we didn't see them at all. Two destroyers and a light cruiser were sent to find us but were late in starting because they had to collect survivors from other British warships sunk earlier the day before in Colombo. Eventually we saw the masts of three ships on the horizon and everyone cheered. Then someone said "They're Japanese". We immediately thought of being bustled on board, beaten and kicked to death, prisoners of war and that didn't help, but we soon realised that they were ours when we saw the White Ensign flying. They were *HMS Panther* a fairly old destroyer, *HMS Enterprise* a light cruiser and *HMS Paladin* a modern destroyer. The *Paladin* found us. The other ships picked up the survivors from the *Cornwall*.

They came in as close as they could, let their nets down over the ship's side and everybody was on the main deck ready to help with ropes. Some of them dived overboard into the water to help the injured climb the netting. I was able to get up there on my own. I was glad to be standing on something solid after so long in the water. The crew of the *Paladin* hosed us down with warm water and soap. We stripped off and they helped us to clean up. We were like black men with thick oil in our eyes, faces and hair; you wouldn't have recognised anybody. Our shipmates on the *Paladin* got us cleaned up and brought us their own clothes and something to put on our feet. If they had it, they gave it to us and our old clothes were thrown overboard. We were parched so we were given drinks of lemonade and soon after that, a rum issue was ordered. The *Paladin* suspected there were Jap subs around and started dropping depth charges. That really frightened us after our ordeal in the water. The following morning we were making our way back towards the fleet when they transferred the wounded men, including me, to another ship that took us back to Male in the Maldives.

We landed at Male where the Navy had organised wooden bunks from somewhere and we had a bunk each. It was there that at last I met up again with my old friend aboard ship, Tom Shirley, who had saved my life in the boiler room. He said "There's a little canteen just down the road if you want some fags, I've been down there but I haven't got any money". I had my web belt with a little bit of money because it could be thieved, even aboard ship. They weren't all so innocent, you know. I said "I've got some money, Tom, what do you want, a pound, ten shillings?" "Ten shillings will be OK", he said. "I'll pay you back as soon as possible" but he added, "I don't have anything on me" (because he had had all his clothes blown off him. He had been badly burned when he caught the blast of a bomb on board ship).

After two days we left the Maldives and Tom and I were both put on a hospital ship, although we didn't see one another. I told Tom afterwards, I had been in the sick bay in bed with shock and bronchitis, in a bit of a state and it wasn't improving. The hospital ship took us to Durban via Madagascar and once there I was taken by ambulance to a hospital outside of Durban which had been a racecourse and pavilion converted for troop distribution to the Middle East.

First Lieut. Geoffrey Grove

Lieut. Grove had been aboard the *Cornwall* but was now chest-deep in water with several others in an overcrowded float. He was concerned about the injured men whom he knew would surely die if they could not be got out of the water as quickly as possible. It was decided therefore to try to join up with the motor boat where it was hoped there might be a doctor. It took two hours to pull the quarter of a mile between the float and the motor boat and Lieut. Grove recalled how the Major (Trailen), a stoker, a seaman named Galbraith who had survived the sinking of the *Prince of Wales* and he took it in turns, adding 'At times we thought it would never come any closer'. When they did finally make it, all the thanks they got for bundling their injured shipmates aboard was curses for being clumsy and aggravating their pain. But it was no easy job and Lieut. Groves and the others had done the best they could.

CHAPTER 7

Nagumo Follows up with Trincomalee and More Ships are Sunk

Following the attack on Colombo on 5th April and the sinking of the two cruisers, *Cornwall* and *Dorsetshire*, later that same day Nagumo regrouped his fleet and moved south-eastwards where he maintained a distance of 500 miles to avoid being spotted by Allied patrolling aircraft. He refuelled his ships on the 7th and the following day, turned north-west, ready to launch a surprise attack on Trincomalee at dawn on 9th April from a distance of 200 miles.

We were completely unaware what Nagumo's next move might be but suspected it might be Trincomalee. The depleted Hurricane and Fulmar Squadrons continued to stand by, steeling themselves each day ready for the next raid. Day after day went by until the Wednesday afternoon of 8th April when a Catalina of No.240 Squadron piloted by Flying Officer Round spotted the enemy fleet 500 miles east of Dondra Head. An enemy fighter approached the flying boat but as there was plenty of cloud cover Round dived into it, from where he safely returned to his base at Koggala, arriving late at night. The mystery of the whereabouts of the Japanese was solved but more importantly their likely intentions could now be deduced as well. Their objective had to be Trincomalee. The island's defences were put on full alert and the order given to clear Trincomalee harbour of all ships, except for the monitor *Erebus* which had been launched in 1916 and was to remain as a gun platform with her large 15-inch gun, and the merchant ship *Sagaing*.

At this time, 1942, Trincomalee, in direct contrast to Colombo, did not have a large urban population. Apart from its dockyard area, it was little more than a large, scattered village with a predominantly Tamil population. Clustered around the many bays and inlets in the harbour, including Koddiar Bay, were tiny fishing communities. An attack by enemy bombers would have caused very few civilian casualties. In fact, there was very little to attack in Trincomalee, other than the dockyard.

The most important of the few ships anchored in Trincomalee harbour at this time was the aircraft carrier *Hermes* under the command of Captain Richard Onslow. It had arrived only four days earlier after leaving the main fleet. This 10,850 ton aircraft carrier was commissioned in 1923 and was the first Royal Navy ship to be specially designed as such. Initially she had been designed to carry 20 aircraft but during a refit at the end of 1934 *Hermes* was fitted with a catapult and a second

HMS Hermes.

lift, which reduced the number of aircraft that could be carried to 15. For the past few months she had been undertaking regular patrols between Simonstown, Mombasa, Mauritius, the Persian Gulf and the Maldives, and had been scheduled to sail to Australia to help in her defence if the Japanese had moved southwards. A change of plans now included her in the Madagascar operations due to start the following month.

Aboard the *Hermes* the recall signal was hoisted for the benefit of those ashore and every measure taken to get the message to them quickly, but it was 7pm before she weighed anchor and darkness was falling as she left for the open sea with her escort, the *Vampire* under the command of Lieut. Commander W.T.A. Moran. Such was the speed at which *Hermes* had to put to sea she did not have the time to take her 12 Fairey Swordfish Mark I aircraft of No. 814 Naval Air Squadron aboard, except for the two which were under repair in her hanger. They remained at China Bay so consequently she and the other ships had no air cover. This made the carrier extremely vulnerable to air attack if spotted, so her plan was to steam southwards, keeping well clear of the coast to place sufficient distance between herself and Trincomalee. By adopting this tactic it was thought she would be well clear of the

HMS Vampire.

Japanese line of approach. Accompanying these two ships was the tanker, *British Sergeant*, the corvette, *Hollyhock* and the depot ship, *Athelstone*.

As soon as the naval authorities received warning of the impending attack on Trincomalee, and given the location and size of the force, they dispatched 11 Blenheim bombers from the racecourse airstrip to attack Nagumo's fleet, the first time the carriers had ever been threatened. At 8am Squadron-Leader Ault, the senior flight commander, prepared to lead the Blenheims of No.11 Squadron into the air to strike back at the Japanese. By 8.20am the bombers were airborne and formed up into two flights, but two of the Blenheims developed engine trouble almost straight away and had to return to base; the remaining nine flew on, climbing steadily. It seemed like a pitifully small force compared to the huge armadas the Japanese were using against us.

There was no question of a fighter escort to accompany them because the Hurricanes had nowhere near the range that the Zeros had and the attack would have to be made in broad daylight against overwhelming odds, so the pilots must have known they would be lucky to return. It was something they were used to, having been undertaking this sort of operation since the beginning of the war, according to Gordon Wallace in his book *Carrier Observer*. After leaving the east coast behind them the aircraft passed north of the *Hermes'* position, making for the area from which Flying Officer Thomas had made his dawn sighting. By 10am Ault's Blenheims were in position and after circling for some fifteen minutes, finally saw the whole Japanese fleet spread out over

A Blenheim bomber similar to those that took part in this attack.

several square miles of ocean below them. They were spotted by the Japanese who at first identified six of the aircraft as being Wellington bombers and a number of Zero fighters went up to meet them, pouncing with a murderous rate of fire. Undeterred, the Blenheims went into a formation bombing run at a height of 11,000 ft, their bombs straddled the *Akagi* and according to Japanese records, it was damaged by a near-miss. Unfortunately the Blenheims caused little damage to the rest of the carriers.

Aboard Vice-Admiral Nagumo's flagship *Akagi*, the alarm sounded as huge columns of water shot into the air on either side of the vessel. The first bombs straddled the carrier, slightly ahead but not hitting her. It is a tribute to the Blenheim crews that they managed to drop their bombs so accurately in such conditions but with their payload gone, they headed for home hotly pursued by the Zeros. In the action five Blenheims were lost whilst the remaining four were badly damaged.

Shortly after 1pm the four damaged Blenheims returned to the racecourse airstrip; Squadron Leader Ault was not amongst them. Other pilots lost were Flying Officer E. Adcock, Pilot Officer R. Knight, and Sergeants Stevenson and McClennan. Altogether seventeen lives were lost in the attack and although the Japanese suffered no significant damage it was the first time Nagumo's carrier strike force had been attacked either by surface or air forces since Pearl Harbour.

As we now know, Nagumo had planned his attack on Trincomalee for the day after the attack by the Blenheims and as no damage had been sustained by any of his ships during the attack his plan remained unaltered. Take-off time was scheduled for sunrise using the same plan of attack as before, only this time the Japanese were confident of finding the British fleet at anchor. It would definitely be a second Pearl Harbour, only this time with the British Eastern Fleet being the victim. The only difference between this attack and those on Pearl Harbour and Colombo was that it was not taking place on a Sunday morning.

At 6.20am with the early morning sun lighting up the sky behind them, Fuchida's carrier force of three battleships and five carriers including the *Akagi*, *Hiryu* and *Soryu*, which had entered the Bay of

Bengal only a week earlier, launched 91 bombers (Kates) and 38 fighters (Zeros). Two of the Kates were detached to check Colombo harbour whilst a number of Vals stood by, ready to attack the Eastern Fleet should it be found in either harbour. As the two Kates were heading for Colombo, they reported seeing the *Hermes* and the *Vampire* heading south. The Japanese fleet was spread over a distance of about fifteen square miles and the sound of the aircraft engines must have been audible from a great distance. Nagumo hoped once again to achieve total surprise but was unaware he had been sighted by a Catalina flying boat of No. 413 Squadron. Flight Lieut. 'Tommy' Thomas had taken up shadowing duties in 'Y for Yorker' after leaving Koggala and after heading east, sent his first message at 7am but it was an emergency signal which suddenly broke off and contact could not be regained. He was presumed to be another victim of the Zero fighter aircraft.

The stage was now set for Ceylon's second assault. No.261 Squadron's Hurricanes under Squadron Leader A.G. Lewis DFC had been on stand-by since before dawn on the 5th April, having flown many patrols and been scrambled on several occasions since. A satellite airstrip near the coast at Kokkilai, fifteen miles north of Trincomalee, had been hurriedly prepared and a flight kept there during daylight hours. The strip was barely long enough for take-off and already one precious Hurricane had been written off here when a sergeant-pilot overshot and crashed into some trees. In its favour, the tiny airstrip was not likely to be spotted by the Japanese.

A dawn patrol of three Hurricanes from No. 261 Squadron took off from China Bay at 6.35am as strong radar contact picked up at Trincomalee indicated something was coming in from the east at a range of 30 miles. Six more of our fighters took off at 7.10am led by Flight-Lieut. Cleaver and five minutes later, another six under Flight-Lieut. Marshall were scrambled from Kokkilai. Six Fulmars of No.273 Squadron, although hopelessly mismatched against the Zeros, also took off to join the fray. The fight was on but this time we had the advantage of our fighters being in the air, ready to meet the incoming raiders. Fuchida later said, "Enemy radar must have detected our approach, for Hurricane fighters came out to intercept before we reached the target". The three defending fighter sections fought hard to get at the bombers but had to engage in dog-fights with the Zeros instead. The battle raged from around 8,000 ft to 22,000 ft.

Flight-Lieut. D. Fulford who won the DFC that day, described the action. "I took off at 0652 hrs with Flight-Sergeant Rawnsley and Sergeant Walton forming Emerald Section and climbed to a height of 15,000 feet. I had been told to fly out on a vector of 100 degrees to meet a strong plot of aircraft flying thirty miles from the coast. I flew behind some cumulus cloud to protect my eyes from the sun and almost immediately sighted the enemy aircraft. They were at a height of 15,000 ft., flying due west, straight towards the harbour. I saw two formations of twin-engine bombers, each comprising of two groups of seven in line astern, escorted by a number of Navy O's.

"A moment later I sighted another similar formation about a mile behind. The escorting fighters were not in a definite formation but spread out all around the bombers. I saw the sun glinting on their perspex windscreens above and behind me so I brought the section together into a tight group and we climbed to the north behind some cloud. I climbed to a height of 22,000 ft. then turned west until I was over the rear formation. I noticed that several enemy fighters were weaving behind the formation so we dived down and selected one each."

Having taken the greatest of care to get his section into an optimum position, Fulford and his pilots began their attack on the Japanese aircraft and their formation was quickly broken up as the British aircraft relentlessly kept up their assault. Later it was learned that Walton had been shot down and killed. Rawnsley's aircraft was badly damaged and he had to land back at his base with a damaged undercarriage, a manoeuvre hampered by the fact that a Zero followed him down and when Flt.-Lieut. Edsall came over to help him from the damaged aircraft, the Zero opened fire, causing serious injury to both men.

For all the early warning they had, No.261 Squadron did not fare much better than the Colombo-based Squadrons; the odds were simply too great. Eight Hurricanes were shot down and another, apart from

Rawnsley's, was damaged beyond repair. Two sergeants had been killed in the action as well as four others, including the CO. Flying Officer Gregg's Fulmar from No. 273 Squadron also failed to return from the day's operations.

But even with ample warning it seemed that our fighters had not managed to disrupt the Japanese attack. They were seemingly unstoppable. Their bombers reached Trincomalee harbour at 7.20am but were disappointed at not finding the fleet at anchor. Undeterred they attacked what shipping they did find with ruthless efficiency. The *Erebus* was hit many times with heavy casualties among her small crew, and the *Sagaing*, her decks ablaze, had to be beached; the four aircraft she had been carrying were lost in the fires.

There were two anti-aircraft batteries positioned near the dockyard, one manned by Royal Marines and the other by soldiers of the 55th Light AA Regiment. They were effective enough to attract low-level strafing by a couple of Zeros. Military Medals were awarded that day to two of the gunners who with ammunition blazing around them, continued firing their Bofors gun even after two of the gun crew had been killed by Japanese fire.

On the other side of the harbour the China Bay aerodrome had been attacked. We had fighter aircraft in the air but they were nowhere to be seen. They were in fact away to the east intercepting other incoming enemy raiders. It was only those aircraft that were limping home damaged or short of fuel and ammunition that came into contact with the Japanese over Trincomalee. Considerable damage was done at China Bay where a full petrol bowser exploded in flames, an ammunition dump was hit, causing extensive damage to two hangars, and 261's orderly room was totally demolished. One stick of bombs fell between the officers' mess and quarters up on the hill whilst on the ground three men were killed and six wounded. As a parting shot one Japanese pilot deliberately crashed his aircraft into one of the Navy's huge fuel tanks situated to the north of the aerodrome. There were not many of these tanks that were full but the pilot found one that was. It blazed spectacularly for several days. This was two years before the Kamikaze squadrons of suicide pilots were formed, but it is quite clear from contemporary reports that this pilot was in no way under any pressure to carry out this act.

Fuchida's squadrons withdrew from Trincomalee by 8am. We claimed to have destroyed five bombers and six fighters but no evidence of these aircraft has ever been found. It is possible they crashed into the sea, as did some of ours. In finding comparatively little opposition in the attack and being confident they could evade any naval forces sent against them, if such forces really did exist, the Japanese fleet had come in rather closer than they had the previous Sunday. Even though the bombing of the harbour facilities and the airfield had been carried out with due Japanese efficiency, the results hardly justified the scale of the attack. In comparison, more had been achieved by Vice-Admiral Ozawa's smaller carrier force which sank 23 merchant ships on 6th April between Madras and Calcutta, accounting for 112,312 tons.

If Nagumo had anticipated finding and destroying the Eastern Fleet at Trincomalee, he was once again disappointed. If only he had used the long range and speed capabilities of the Zero fighter to make a reconnaissance flight before launching his attack it would have had a different result, but this is a strategy which does not rate too highly in Japanese planning. It must have been galling to Nagumo not to have found the Eastern Fleet where he considered it should be but then two of his Kates spotted the *Hermes* and the *Vampire* steering in a southerly direction and suspecting the Eastern Fleet could not be far away, he ordered a second strike to get ready before the Trincomalee sortie had all returned. His initial reaction to the report was of alarm but his main concern was that his ships might be in danger of attack and many of his protective fighter aircraft were already engaged a considerable distance away from their carriers. He ordered his aircraft to open their throttles and head for home at full speed. Alas, he did not know that the *Hermes* did not have a single serviceable aircraft aboard her.

Nagumo was now in a vulnerable position with no air cover as he awaited the return of his first strike force. He turned his carriers on to a south-easterly heading, into the wind and held it until all the aircraft were safely aboard. Nagumo must have been relieved to complete the recovery of the remains of the first strike force. He then altered course due south. But he still did not know whether the anticipated attack would be by either shore- or carrier-based aircraft; he was still unaware that the *Hermes* had no aircraft aboard. As the last of the Japanese aircraft returning from Trincomalee were landing on their respective ships, those already down were being refuelled and re-armed in case the reserve force failed to sink the *Hermes*. Above them was a full combat patrol on alert. Over the course of the next hour much was set to happen as over fifty dive-bombers and twenty fighters took to the air in perfect weather conditions, led by Lt.Cmdr. Egusa from the *Hiryu*, in pursuit of the *Hermes* and the *Vampire*.

Then, something quite bizarre happened. An ancient native sailing-boat, the *Sederhana Djohanis*, with sixteen British officers, a Malayan and a Chinaman on board sailed unexpectedly into the area of the Japanese fleet. She had been commandeered at Padang in Sumatra and spent many days at sea making slow progress westwards. On one occasion they had been sighted by a Japanese aircraft which had made a half-hearted attack on them. They believed they were approaching friendly waters but the Japanese aircraft flew in for a second attack. They were disheartened to see two Japanese tankers heading eastwards and concluded that Ceylon had been overrun as had Malaya and the Dutch East Indies. The merchantman *Anglo-Canadian,* en route to Bombay, spotted the *Sederhana Djohanis* and took the survivors aboard. As the *Sederhana Djohanis* was still afloat and as such could have posed a danger to shipping, the *Anglo-Canadian* sank her by shell fire. By the morning of April 19 the *Anglo-Canadian* was at anchor in Bombay Roads, India along with dozens of other merchant ships and the entire Eastern Fleet. The survivors were firstly transferred to *HMS Formidable* and later to the *Warspite* for debriefing. Eventually they returned to the UK in the next available troopship.

After the war it was realized that the *Sederhana Djohanis* ordeal was all the more successful because another identical prauw which must have left the Padang area soon after the *Sederhana Djohanis* was stopped near Ceylon by a Japanese tanker [or its escort] and all aboard were taken prisoner.

At the time of the attack on Trincomalee the *Hermes* and the other ships in her group were some 65 miles to the south of Ceylon, and believing it would be safe to return once the raid had finished started to steam back into port. Having won mastery of the skies over Trincomalee but finding little to attack, Nagumo's bombers were now searching for secondary worthwhile targets, and this was when a seaplane from the battleship *Haruna* came across the *Hermes*. Aboard the *Hermes* Captain Onslow realized he had been spotted and expected to be attacked at any moment. With little to retaliate with, he turned back towards Trincomalee, moving obliquely shoreward at the same time, hoping to come within range of fighter aircraft protection.

Hermes' ship's company was called to action stations and just before daylight her four Bofors guns, her Oerlikons and the two 4-inch guns on her stern were manned but her main 5.5-inch armament below the flight deck could not be elevated high enough against attacking aircraft. With such little opposition, Egusa's pilots achieved an incredible percentage of direct hits with their bombs. It was noticeable that more often than not, flames and smoke billowed upwards rather than the slender plumes of water from near-misses. Such accuracy was unparalleled, even in future operations.

The Japanese pilots were completely surprised to find the *Hermes* had absolutely no air cover. The dive-bombers went into their tried and tested attack position of line astern and plunged headlong into the attack. The Japanese pilots knew by now, by adopting this line of approach, ships could not bring their guns to bear on them. Lieut. Brimble, Second Gunnery Officer on the *Hermes*, recalled how the ship kept altering helm every few minutes, twisting and turning, desperately trying to deflect the pilots' aim, but unlike a destroyer, the aircraft carrier is not entirely suitable for this sort of manoeuvre. *Hermes* opened fire on the incoming aircraft but her guns seemed to have little effect. The Japanese came in so low they were in serious danger of being blown apart by the blast of their own bombs. As someone later commented, "We were in the look-out position some 120 feet above the flight deck and at times, some of the enemy aircraft swept by well below us".

During the attack several of *Hermes'* gunners were killed and their guns put out of action. The bombs dropped by the Japanese were delay-fused and after penetrating the flight deck, exploded in the hanger beneath or entered the engine room. Suddenly the attack was called off and the aircraft took off towards the distant shore. *Hermes* herself continued in the same direction for a good half-an-hour. It is thought she was hurriedly trying to get into shallow waters where the submarines that were thought to be in the vicinity would have less of an opportunity of attacking with torpedoes. As the crews desperately tried to repair the damage, an estimated seventy aircraft were spotted flying at a great height overhead. At first the sailors thought they were RAF planes but wishful thinking soon turned to disappointment when they realized the aircraft were Japanese using the same tactics as the previous group, coming in one after another in a constant stream, so that as one stick of bombs exploded, the next one was already in the air from the following plane. The second rain of bombs fell thick and fast and the ship was soon ablaze from stem to stern, sinking slowly, but still the Japanese aircraft continued the attack. Finally the order, "Every man for himself" was given and a few moments later the bridge received a direct hit. It is believed this is when Captain Onslow died. No one in that area survived.

By now the doomed ship was just eight miles from the shore and the crew was leaping into the sea. The bombing had destroyed most of the ships' boats and life-saving equipment. Her flight deck was by now at a crazily steep angle, throwing the remaining survivors into the sea. Five miles out the *Hermes* finally plunged beneath the waves into thirty fathoms of water, still fiercely blazing. At the start of the attack Captain Onslow had radioed repeatedly for air cover but at the China Bay airstrip they were in no position to help or even listen to his request. Only the Japanese picked up the signals from the *Hermes*. Captain Onslow's calls were eventually picked up at Ratmalana and

HMS Hermes sinking, as seen by the Japanese pilots.

eight Fulmars of Nos. 803 and 806 Squadrons took off at about 10am to try to help. They headed out eastwards across the island but arrived in time to see the final stages of the attack. Sub. Lt. Metcalfe later recalled he saw 'the carrier and the destroyer lying stopped, like a couple of beetles being attacked by a swarm of ants'. As he dived to attack, he caught a glimpse of a huge ball of flame shooting up from the carrier. He then became heavily involved with two Vals attacking him from either quarter, and realising that whichever way he turned he was done for, he stood his Fulmar on its tail, and since full-throttle would not be enough power to get him away, he pulled the boost cut-out and climbed clear of his adversaries. By the time he had levelled out, *Hermes* had sunk and the enemy aircraft were dispersing. As there was nothing he could do for the survivors, Metcalfe flew on to China Bay where he managed to land amongst the debris from the earlier attack. In this incident two Fulmars were shot down and despite the Japanese claiming they had lost no aircraft, our pilots were adamant they had shot down four Vals and damaged two more. As the elated Japanese pilots were turning away, the eight Fulmars promised earlier as air cover for the *Hermes* arrived on the scene and plunged into a futile revenge attack on the Japanese pilots. It was a brief engagement in which two of the Fulmars were shot down. Soon after 11am a jubilant Lieut-Commander Egusa led his formations back to the carriers, leaving many survivors floundering in the sea with the smoke from the *Hermes* lingering over the scene. Of aircraft losses in this attack, both gunners from the *Hermes* and Fulmar crews claimed to have shot down an undisclosed number of enemy aircraft but Japanese sources do not mention any losses.

The attack had commenced at 10.35am yet by 10.50am *Hermes* was dead in the water, a gutted, flaming hull with her sides shattered and her deck ripped to splinters; five minutes later she capsized and sank. It was followed by the *Vampire* shortly after and it took the Japanese pilots just ten minutes to break the ship's back, thus sinking her too. The *Vampire*, still close by, had seen it all before for she was with the *Prince of Wales* and the *Repulse* when they were sunk and had taken many of those survivors aboard. This time however, she was not spared and received several direct hits. She sank even closer inshore with the loss of eight men including her captain. Of the complement on the *Hermes*, 19 officers and 283 ratings were killed. The wreck of the *Hermes* was found sixty-three years later, in 2006 when divers attached the White Ensign to the rusting hull. The wreck of the *Vampire* has never been found.

Despite their ordeal, the survivors from the *Hermes* fared better than their shipmates from the *Dorsetshire* and the *Cornwall*. Soon after the sinking, a small hospital ship, the *Vita*, coming up from the south, appeared on the scene. She spent the rest of the morning and early afternoon searching for survivors from the various ships that had been sunk. When satisfied there were no more, she turned south and headed for Colombo. She rescued approximately 600 survivors from the two ships and took them firstly to Colombo, and later to Kandy, for recuperation.

There was however, one group of seven seamen the *Vita* missed. They were all from the *Hermes* and after the ship had gone down, they decided to swim the five miles to shore together. When the *Vita* started picking up survivors they thought she was a Japanese vessel and swam on, away from her. They refused to leave any stragglers behind and swam on, making slow progress. It was almost dusk when they reached a navigational buoy just outside the harbour at Batticaloa.

Exhausted by the long swim, they secured themselves to the buoy for the night and stayed there until a local fishing boat came out to take them ashore.

Having now lost three of our most important ships Admiral Somerville sent a signal to the Admiralty informing them he was not prepared to send another warship to this area without fighter aircraft protection.

But what became of the other ships that had accompanied the *Hermes* when she left Trincomalee? Earlier, at 4pm the order had been given for the tanker, the *British Sergeant* that had been discharging fuel at China Bay, the Royal Fleet Auxiliary Ship *Athelstone*, the cable ship *Hecla*, a new Flower class corvette, the *Hollyhock* and a single merchant ship, the *Sagaing* to up anchor and disperse out to sea. Only one warship was to remain in the harbour throughout the emergency, the old monitor *Erebus*, launched in 1916, which was to be used as a gun platform for her large 15-inch guns. The *Athelstone* and the *Hollyhock* left together but the *British Sergeant* left alone. The ships fanned out, hoping they would disappear from Japanese view, but with the benefit of hindsight about the thoroughness of Japanese aerial reconnaissance, it might have been better to have left the ships where they were. Lt. Cdr. Egusa's second strike force came across the *Hollyhock*, the *Athelstone* and the *British Sergeant* whilst looking for the *Hermes* and at 9.22am a number of Vals attacked and sunk them.

While the day's engagements were being fought on the east coast of Ceylon, Admiral Somerville, far away at Addu Atoll, decided that his slow and out-dated battle squadron was a liability based at Addu Atoll where there was little, or no, defence against an attack on it in the harbour. He decided therefore to withdraw to the naval base at Kilindini near Mombasa. He also decided to move his fast squadron, Force A, northwards from Addu Atoll to Bombay where it could at least act as a deterrent against the Japanese operating in the Indian Ocean. The Bombay posting was not to last for long because unbeknown to Somerville, Nagumo's attack on Trincomalee was the culmination of the Japanese operations in the Indian Ocean, after which they gradually withdrew, leaving only Admiral Hara's two carriers of the 5th Division to go to Truk in the Pacific to cover the final phase of the invasion of New Guinea. Having cost the Allies over 100,000 tons in shipping losses and caused the British to suspend all shipping operations between Burma and India, Admiral Nagumo set sail for action in the Pacific with his carrier strike force which had by now steamed more than 50,000 miles since attacking Pearl Harbour, had won many battles and all with the loss of only a dozen aircraft. Nagumo's ships needed repairs and maintenance, and his aircrews, rest and regrouping. The Eastern Fleet had not made a single offensive move against the Japanese, something Somerville could not possibly have relished. Churchill later reflected that when the German High Seas Fleet fought the British Grand Fleet at Jutland in 1916, Admiral Jellicoe had the chance to lose the war in the course of a single afternoon. Might not Admiral Somerville have had in mind that, with the Eastern Fleet in his charge, he had been placed in the same unenviable position?

Somerville's reluctance to make an offensive move against the Japanese was something he was not particularly proud of but he was unwilling to risk his fleet against the might of the Japanese. Somerville had very nearly had the opportunity for revenge after one of his carrier reconnaissance aircraft spotted Zero fighters some 300 miles south of Ceylon but Nagumo was not willing to commit his carrier force to a night action which could have been a disaster so he set off eastwards. The next day, when he resumed the hunt westwards, Nagumo discovered that Somerville did not want to engage with the Japanese during daylight hours when the odds were stacked against him so for the next forty hours the two fleets played a game of cat and mouse, each hoping to catch the other out, but they never came to blows.

Meanwhile, Nagumo had sent his tankers and supply ships back to their base. Ozawa could find no more targets in the Bay of Bengal and both task forces retired to an area between the Andaman and Nicobar Islands. Ceylon's trials were over, something not fully appreciated by the islanders at the time. There was a general sense of elation, for although our fighter aircraft had faced a severe onslaught, the morale of the survivors must equally have suffered a severe mauling as it was brought sharply into focus that the Japanese had far superior resources to ours. Ceylon was left with no naval forces. It soon became known that the *Hermes* and the *Vampire* had been sunk off the east coast, but the fate of the *Cornwall* and the *Dorsetshire* was known only to a very few people. So many of our ships had been sunk and no one was sure where the fleet was anymore, but everyone was confident it was close at hand. What no one knew was that the Eastern Fleet had already been ordered to retire from the area around Ceylon and not to return to its harbours under any circumstances. Whereas just a week previously invasion had seemed to be a distinct possibility, being the inevitable result of every Japanese action so far, the general mood now was that the Japanese had been soundly repulsed and there was understandable optimism.

In his book *The Turn of the Tide* (1957) Arthur Bryant was of the opinion that back in London on the 10th April the Chiefs of Staff were now concerned with trying to save India from the Japanese. They too had yet to appreciate that the main threat was over and Churchill was still of the opinion that "until we are able to fight a fleet action, there is no reason why the Japanese should not dominate in the western Indian Ocean". He warned President Roosevelt of 'the immense perils that were now threatening Burma and India', and asked him to send more ships across the Atlantic so that British warships could be sent to reinforce the Eastern Fleet to 'offer some menace to the Japanese' but although Roosevelt was sympathetic to Churchill's plea, he had his own operations planned in the Pacific and could not spare the ships. Roosevelt said he could only send in more bombers to strengthen the defence of India. He gave no hint of an operation that was already being planned to strike back at Japan. It was intended as a propaganda move aimed at boosting American morale but it would also jolt the Imperial General Staff so profoundly, it would change the course of the Pacific War.

Churchill was able to present a more positive stance to President Roosevelt than he was towards his own Cabinet when he said 'I believe that any junction between the Japanese and the Germans is going to take a great deal of doing but realize that the remote prospect of this is something to be watched. In the meantime, as you will have seen in the Press, we have had a good crack at Japan by air and I am hoping that we can make it very difficult for them to keep too many of their big ships in the Indian Ocean.'

CHAPTER 8

The Sequel and Its Aftermath

Following two days at sea, Admiral Somerville put in to Bombay with the much-reduced, faster element of his fleet, where a conference of the naval, army and air forces, together with the civil powers, had been arranged. General Wavell, Commander-in-Chief of India was disillusioned with the situation at sea. He had expected great things of the fleet but his view had been drawn sharply into focus by the knowledge that we had lost all control of the Indian Ocean, except for the area off the African coast. But an ever-optimistic Somerville pointed out that at the very least, the fleet's presence in Indian waters would deter the Japanese from operating against our shipping and he would be following orders by using light force only. As he put it, 'I shall have to lie low in one sense, but be pretty active in another'.

The Indian part of Convoy WS16 arrived at Bombay after an uneventful voyage lasting two months but the reinforcements in this convoy were not of the right sort to relieve the current situation. Wavell demanded more aircraft and protested that present naval forces were insufficient to protect either India or Ceylon from possible invasion. It seemed highly likely to him the Japanese, having probed our defences, would soon return with troops. He unfairly contrasted No.11 Squadron's efforts with the huge raid then being mustered against Germany by Bomber Command, and questioned whether the Chiefs of Staff Committee were serious in their desire to retain India. He got little sympathy; we were now committed to a new plan, Operation Ironclad, the occupation of Diego Suarez, a base in northern Madagascar together with the occupation of as much territory as would be needed to secure the unhindered use of the harbour there, for which all available reinforcements were being diverted, – and for which Wavell's resources in India were to be depleted even more. With the Mediterranean closed to us and all materials and reinforcements having to be routed round the Cape of Good Hope, Madagascar, situated between the Mozambique Channel and the more open eastward sea route, commanded the shipping lanes along which everything had to pass.

The Chiefs of Staff considered the immediate threat to India and Ceylon by both sea and by land had receded, as did Wavell later on, but before the Indian Ocean could return to its normal peaceful state one final blow was to be delivered against the Japanese. A Lockheed Hudson aircraft from Akyab on the northern coast of Burma, whilst carrying out a standard reconnaissance patrol over Port Blair in the Andaman Islands on 11th April spotted nine Japanese flying boats at anchor. Three days later two Hudsons flew in to attack them, sinking one and leaving two ablaze. On the 18th they returned and logged a claim of two destroyed and three damaged. This time however, Zero fighters came to their rescue and shot down one of the Hudsons.

On the same day, the Ceylon part of Convoy WS16 in the troopship *Devonshire*, arrived at Colombo but with recent events still fresh in everyone's mind, a careful anti-submarine watch was kept. The ocean was empty however and nothing disturbed the glassy, blue surface, not even the occasional flying fish of which there were plenty here. A pall of black smoke still hung over the harbour at Colombo where the *Hector* continued to burn. The docks were deserted and most of the town's population had gone away. It was to be some weeks later before they began to slowly trickle back. It seemed like the Japanese were far away, but no one really knew for sure.

In his book, *The Most Dangerous Moment*, Michael Tomlinson recalled how upon the *Devonshire*'s arrival at Colombo, because there were no dock workers, the troops had to row themselves ashore in the ship's boats. Few of his comrades had left Europe before so to them it seemed like they had been dropped into a strange tropical land where the climate was hot and humid. For the past two months the troops had been confined to the ship with only two brief excursions ashore. There was a general air of there being less of an emergency here than there had at Singapore but everyone thought the Japanese would return in the near future so the troops prepared to retaliate if needed.

General Wavell accompanied Admiral Somerville back to Colombo in the *Warspite* for discussions with Admiral Layton and the other service chiefs, the Eastern Fleet then made for the Seychelles from where they steamed on to Kilindini near Mombasa, and Vice-Admiral Nagumo and his fleet, having refuelled at Singapore, anticipated heading for home waters. It had been a fortnight since the alarm had first been raised in Ceylon. Although not fully fulfilled, Nagumo had completed his task by driving the British Eastern Fleet from the Indian Ocean to the relative safety of East Africa; Burma, the Andamans and Sumatra were protected from British naval raids; it is little wonder that everyone regarded the Japanese as being invincible.

From a naval perspective there was now a total vacuum in the Bay of Bengal and the Indian Ocean as the focus of the war with Japan switched to the Pacific where the Americans would make the Japanese pay dearly for their earlier triumphs. It was time for the Japanese to implement their promise made by Admiral Nomura to the Germans, to operate off the east coast of Africa. It was admitted the Indian Ocean was of only minor importance to the Japanese and their major fleet units would have to remain in the Pacific to fight the Battle of the Coral Sea and the Battle of Midway. Although the Americans lost many of their battleships in these engagements, Vice-Admiral Nagumo's triumphant carrier strike force was called upon once again but this time it was reduced to an insignificant remnant, a mere shadow of the proud fleet that only two months earlier had approached Ceylon. Many of the highly experienced pilots and crews that had pounded Colombo, Trincomalee, and the ships *Dorsetshire, Cornwall* and *Hermes* were lost in these engagements.

Recriminations were bound to follow the events of April 1942 in the Indian Ocean where we had survived a severe trial in which there was no glory. Churchill's high hopes of our Eastern Fleet had been dashed. Instead of forcing discretion on the Japanese and calling a halt to their westward expansion plans, the fleet had been bustled ignominiously off the scene with unexpected major losses. Churchill wasted no time in criticizing the Admiralty, making them the scapegoat. Why, he wanted to know, did the Japanese carriers have many more aircraft than ours? Why were our aircrews always said to be untrained? Was Somerville justified in sending the *Dorsetshire* and the *Cornwall* to Colombo, and the *Hermes* and the *Vampire* to Trincomalee? Was it the right move to order the *Hermes* and other vessels to set sail once an air attack was expected? And how was all this to be explained to Parliament and the country?

The great man demanded answers and would not be fobbed off. Sir Dudley Pound, the First Sea Lord, and the Rt. Hon. A.V. Alexander, the First Lord of the Admiralty both defended Somerville's actions and Pound did his best to deal with all the points raised. He confirmed that throughout, the Admiralty had maintained their confidence in Admiral Somerville's judgment but now he had to bear the brunt of the criticism. It was clear he had done his best to obey his orders and dealt with the Chiefs of Staff Committee's rapidly changing attitudes which in the short space of ten days had changed from aggressive intent to full flight, followed by a complete abandonment of all initiative in the Indian Ocean.

When addressing the House of Commons, Churchill said, '… I cannot make any statement about the strength of the Forces at Admiral Somerville's disposal, or of the reasons which led him to make the dispositions of his fleet for which he was responsible. Nothing in these dispositions, or the consequences which followed upon them, have in any way weakened the confidence of the Admiralty in his judgement.' Upon hearing this, Somerville wryly commented, 'It was perhaps unfortunate that the announcement of my appointment to the Eastern Fleet should have come at a time when the PM had to say that in spite of serious losses in the operations off Ceylon, the Government had not lost confidence in me.'

The major charge against Somerville was that he needlessly lost the *Hermes* and the cruisers *Dorsetshire* and *Cornwall* in the face of orders "not to stick his neck out". The Admiralty placed the blame for their loss fairly and squarely on his shoulders. This had been the one major decision Somerville seems to have taken without consulting anyone, possibly to safeguard these ships as quickly as possible, but as we now know, it had the opposite effect. The Admiralty concluded when no Japanese ships had appeared by 2nd April that the alarm had been a false alert and on the strength of this hasty conclusion, Somerville's orders to the three ships to return to Ceylon had cost the Eastern Fleet dearly.

To Somerville's credit he would not hear of any criticism of the part the RAF had played in the engagement and strongly refuted the accusation there was insufficient liaison between the two services. It was not as close as it should have been but Ceylon had never been considered as a possible theatre of war until a few days before the Japanese fleet appeared over the horizon. He made no bones about his degree of responsibility for the losses incurred and argued that with what little the RAF had, the airmen had acquitted themselves well. Ceylon's defensive strategy had literally been thrown together from every quarter and had hardly the time to settle before the Japanese were upon them.

Another important factor was the extreme secrecy which had been maintained over the existence of the base at Addu Atoll. Once the Eastern Fleet was at sea, radio silence had to be strictly observed by every ship which prevented any sort of close liaison with Ceylon. No one can question the wisdom of this but it did have serious repercussions. Aircrews flying from Ceylon were told only that our fleet "was in the vicinity". No one was told anything more specific than this, and because the *Formidable* and the *Indomitable*, both with a full complement of aircraft, were with the Eastern Fleet, there was every likelihood their aircraft would be encountered. The Ceylon-based flyers expected this, with the unfortunate result that enemy aircraft were not recognized as such by the Fleet Air Arm Fulmars or by Bradshaw in his Catalina in the early hours of Easter Sunday.

Of the decision to move the *Hermes*, the First Sea Lord maintained it was the right decision to make in the circumstances but it was simply bad luck that an enemy aircraft that was reconnoitring Colombo detected her when she was well clear of Trincomalee. As to why the Japanese carriers had more aircraft than we did, was in their Lordships' opinion, because their crews would put up with cramped quarters which our aircrews would not tolerate. For our senior service with its long, proud traditions, it had been a shattering loss of face to have to retire from such an important sphere of operations without having engaged the enemy and without a single offensive move having been made. The battle for Ceylon had been predominantly an air battle and it clearly demonstrated the need for an efficient carrier-borne air force.

Even when facing so many accusations and counter-accusations, Somerville knew more than anyone else what mortal danger his fleet had been in. But not once did he make a single gesture to betray his deep anxiety. The fleet's trust in him was unquestioning and nothing was done to impair it. Ever since sailing from Colombo, Somerville had deliberately fostered the myth of him being confident and imperturbable. If morale was to be kept high the fact that a British fleet was seemingly avoiding confrontation with the enemy had to be made to look like a normal temporary strategic move with nothing shameful about it.

It is hard to say with any exactitude what the Japanese losses were. The Japanese Imperial Headquarters issued a bulletin following the attack on Colombo in which it is stated they had lost five aircraft and as far as can be seen, no further bulletins were issued covering future operations. Another source which includes other nearby operations, gives the number as seventeen aircraft and about 30 men. Of the two sets of figures, this latter set is possibly nearer the true figure, though it is likely only those lost to direct enemy action are included. Commander Eiziro Suzuki who flew with the 2nd Flying Corps aboard the carriers *Soryu* and *Hiryu* during the Ceylon operation refutes this figure of 17 aircraft entirely, saying it was a gross exaggeration issued by the Royal Navy. Whatever the real number was, it seems that Japanese losses in this Operation were comparatively modest. In comparison, including the civilians, we lost 1,030 people. This does not include those who were injured or those who died later due to those injuries.

British losses

2 8-inch cruisers (*Dorsetshire* and *Cornwall*) – 425 men killed

1 aircraft carrier (*Hermes*) – 302 men killed

2 destroyers (*Tenedos* and *Vampire*) – 23 men killed

1 corvette (*Hollyhock*) – 4 men killed

1 armed merchant cruiser – 4 men killed

Casualties on the *Erebus* and *Lucia* – 10 men killed

23 merchant ships totalling 135,689 tons – 90 men killed

3 Catalina flying boats – 19 men killed and 6 taken as prisoners of war

6 Swordfish torpedo-bombers – 5 men killed

17 Hurricane fighters – 12 pilots killed

5 Blenheim medium bombers – 17 men killed

6 Fulmar fleet fighters – 12 airmen killed

3 men killed on the ground at China Bay

2 members of the 55th LAA Battery killed

17 killed in the naval dockyard at Trincomalee

85 civilians killed in Colombo

To these losses must be added the damage done to the two airfields, Colombo harbour, the railway workshops, the oil installations and civilian property.

For all their easily won successes, the Japanese gained no strategic or tactical advantages from the Ceylon operation. They may have even squandered, though to a lesser extent than Churchill claimed, valuable energy and resources which would have been better committed to their more crucial operations in the Pacific. Had they wanted to return to Ceylon with an invasion force, they could have landed almost unopposed. Our fleet had retired, our air cover was all but destroyed, and essential civilian labour had fled. We were no longer in a position to defend the island if the Japanese chose to press their advantage and invade.

Our Chiefs of Staff had dropped all pretence at disputing command of the sea and air in the Indian Ocean. The Admiralty had sent a signal to Admiral Layton warning him that a full-scale attack on Ceylon was likely and there was no hope of immediate reinforcements being sent. But the Japanese, surprisingly to all, did not return as expected. The Japanese Imperial High Command had decided the time was no longer right and sufficient forces were not available. They had already taken on more than they could comfortably handle in the east. Further conquests were now entirely out of the question. The effect on morale, at a time when we had few reasons for rejoicing, was out of all proportion to the actual situation, but no less real for all that. As the days passed and the threat to Ceylon diminished, the illusion of victory started to emerge and gain in strength. The rest of the world saw this as a sign that the Japanese had been repulsed for the first time since their attack on Pearl Harbour. In Ceylon the elation that was felt about the events of April 1942 could never be eradicated.

The British Eastern Fleet returned to Ceylon on 4th September 1943, moving its' headquarters once again to Colombo, but this time it was scarcely recognizable as the fleet that had retreated to Africa eighteen months previously. Urgent needs in other, more active and important areas had whittled away all the larger ships and at first, no aircraft carriers or battleships could be spared. Later the *Queen Elizabeth* and the *Valiant* formed the nucleus of the fleet at Trincomalee. Admiral Somerville retained command of the fleet long enough to see it take offensive action against the oil installations at Sabaing and Palembang after which he handed over command to Admiral Sir Bruce Fraser. After his retirement from the navy Somerville became Lord Lieutenant of Somerset and died in 1949. When the British Pacific Fleet was formed and it helped the Americans as they closed in on Japan, both the *Formidable* and the *Indomitable* took part in the action. Both were struck by Kamikaze suicide bombers but sustained only slight damage to their steel decks. The *Warspite*, the *Erebus* and "the four Rs" all took part in the D-Day landings at Walcheren in the south of France and survived the war. They later finished their days at the ship breakers' yard.

Of Vice-Admiral Nagumo's fleet, every single vessel was sunk before the end of the war. Within two months of the attack on Trincomalee three of the five aircraft carriers were sunk in the Battle of Midway. The other two were lost in 1944 in separate actions. The cruisers *Chikuma* and *Abukama* were lost at the same time in the Battle of Leyte Gulf. The battleships *Hiei* and *Kirishina* were sunk off Guadalcanal in November 1942 and the *Kongo* was torpedoed by an American submarine two years later. During the last month of the war the *Haruna* was blasted by American bombers whilst at anchor at the naval base of Kure. Ozawa's ships did not last long either. The light carrier *Ryujo* was sunk off the Solomon Islands in August 1942 and three of his cruisers were amongst the heavy losses incurred at Leyte Gulf.

Although Ceylon was no longer under threat from the Japanese, a few of her aircraft did occasionally fly over the island. They were mostly Kawanishi Type 1 Flying Boats known as Emilys, huge four-engine planes, probably on reconnaissance trips to keep check on the Eastern Fleet. The flights generally took place on full-moon nights and one of these aircraft dropped a few bombs harmlessly on the east coast. By this time we had a small flight of radar-equipped Beaufighters on stand-by at the time of each full moon. Two of the Emilys were shot down and there were no survivors from either aircraft although later some bodies were recovered from the sea.

At this time a message was received at the China Bay RAF Station that the remains of an aircraft had been found in a remote part of the jungle some miles to the south of Koddiar Bay. A search party set off hoping to find another enemy flying boat but when they got to the site they found it was a Fulmar that had been missing since the attack on Trincomalee eighteen months earlier. At least the search party was able to give the remains of the pilot and observer a decent burial.

As the Americans started to make preparations for their advance on to the Japanese mainland, the Japanese forces looked to defending their homeland and from then on no major Japanese forces ever entered the Indian Ocean again, except for a brief foray between the Cocos Islands and Australia in March 1944. Although major Japanese warships were no longer active in the Indian Ocean, their submarines continued to be spasmodically active. One of the most notable sinkings was that of the troopship *Khedive Ismail* which sank with a heavy loss of life including a detachment of nurses.

Squadron Leader Birchall and his fellow survivors had been interred in a prisoner-of-war camp after disembarking from the carrier upon which they had initially been held prisoner. After surviving six months at a special interrogation camp at Ojuna where they were starved and beaten daily, Birchall was moved to a work camp near Yokohama. Here he was the Senior Allied Officer among 350 prisoners of war. The Japanese were mercilessly cruel towards their prisoners and Birchall strove courageously for better treatment, particularly for those who were too sick to work. On one occasion he attacked a Japanese sergeant named Ushida who had beaten a man who was too weak to work. In recognition of this brave act, in which he put his own life at risk, Birchall was awarded the OBE.

In later years, Birchall, as Air Commodore commanding the Royal Military College of Canada, revisited Ceylon as a guest of the island's government. One of his former crew, Brian Catlin also went back to Ceylon after the war when he was stationed for a short while at Koggala. He later rose to the rank of Squadron Leader.

Of the key Japanese figures who fought in April 1942, few survived the war or the ensuing war crimes trials. Fuchida survived, having developed appendicitis on the way to Midway where the Americans attacked and crippled his ship, the *Akagi*. The light cruiser *Nagaro* came alongside and took him and Nagumo off, but when jumping between the ships Fuchida broke both of his ankles. After the war he became an instructor at the Imperial Naval War College and was later appointed Air Operations Officer at Combined Fleet Headquarters.

In July 1944, as American Marines took Saipan in the Marianas, Vice-Admiral Chuichi Nagumo took his own life with a pistol with several others of his staff following his example. His body was unrecognized among the others but the evidence is clear enough.

Nagumo was known to be an old fashion Samurai warrior so it was a forgone conclusion that he would never be taken alive.

Vice-Admiral Ozawa succeeded Nagumo as Commander of what was left of the First Air Fleet. He was another of the few Japanese naval officers to live on until after the war. On 29th May, 1945, he accepted a position on the Imperial Japanese Navy General Staff and was the final C-in-C of the Imperial Japanese Navy until the end of the war in September 1945. He refused a promotion to full admiral, and remained as vice-admiral until the final dissolution of the Imperial Japanese Navy.

Commander Shigeru Itaya who had led the fighter aircraft at both Pearl Harbour and Ceylon, was killed in action in 1944, as was Captain Takashige Egusa. Japanese army pilots shot down Itaya accidentally in the bleak fog-bound Kuriles on 24th July and Egusa went down in flames over Saipan.

And so the battle for Ceylon passed into history, just another episode in the war with Japan, and whilst neither side made any significant gains, Japan seems to have come off quite lightly in terms of losses, whilst ours were quite heavy. The one valuable lesson learned was that in future conflicts more emphasis must be placed on carrier-borne aircraft. The days of the capital battleship were numbered.

CHAPTER 9

Victory or Defeat?

When reviewing the events that took place in the Indian Ocean in March and April 1942 seventy-three years on, it is easy to ask was it worth the loss of life incurred in order to have gained so little? Why were the Japanese so successful on so many fronts? Was it simply a case that both the Americans and the British, the major colonial powers in the Far East at that time, were essentially unprepared for war? In direct contrast, the Japanese had been fighting in Manchuria and China for nearly ten years and embraced the necessary strategies for modern warfare. Was it because Japan's national economy revolved around the military and she was simply more prepared for a full-scale assault on the Far East than either the British or Americans were to protect it? Recriminations were bound to follow but likewise there are many questions that need answering.

Many of those involved in the action would, I am sure, say we had simply run away from a superior enemy force, and in his book *The Second World War* Sir Winston Churchill diplomatically described it as 'our having narrowly avoided a major disaster'. It is true to say we survived a severe trial but it was one in which we got no glory. Churchill's high hopes of the Eastern Fleet had been dashed as the Japanese introduced a new way of fighting. Instead of bringing Japan's westward expansion to a halt, the Eastern Fleet had instead been forced to retreat by the Admiralty and Churchill demanded a scapegoat.

Whichever way you see it, it has to be said this was a black page in British naval history. The Royal Navy has a long and proud tradition to uphold but it must have been galling to have to withdraw from such an important theatre of war without having engaged the enemy and without a single offensive move. What made it even worse was that the triumphant enemy was an Asiatic navy, which until then had been seen as someone who emulated western ways, but was never at the forefront of the world's military powers.

Throughout the story of these events there is an underlying impression of British defeatism with no counter-measures seemingly having been put in place against the Japanese fleet who were operating so far from their home bases they would have had considerable difficulties in returning had any of their ships been damaged. But is this a fair assessment? From the moment the presence of the enemy fleet had been suspected there had been an urgent need to block it before the situation got out of hand. Our main weapon with which to do this was the Eastern Fleet but our naval maritime tactics were outdated and far inferior to those of the Japanese. They were in fact, obsolescent.

It was our belief that if traditional surface vessels could not be brought into the action for one reason or another, the carriers *Formidable* and *Indomitable* were at least each equipped with a squadron of Swordfish or Albacore aircraft, though with hindsight, it is difficult to imagine how it was thought these slow, old biplanes could constitute a serious threat against the vastly superior Japanese Zeros which would have greatly outnumbered them anyway. The Japanese had successfully hidden the performance details of the Zero aircraft away from the Western Powers until the very last moment, but by then it was far too late for us to do anything about it. This was a major and decisive factor in the ensuing air battles. Somerville still placed his greatest faith in a night attack from our carriers, which then, as now, was a difficult and dangerous operation. And Churchill himself was still a keen advocate of the battleship.

Whilst the Swordfish and Albacores, the standard aircraft of our Fleet Air Arm, had serious deficiencies and limitations, such as in the case of the Swordfish and a limited flying range, they were far more useful in certain circumstances than the medium bombers such as the Blenheim of which we had just one squadron, No. 11 Squadron, available to strike back at Nagumo's mighty fleet. It was fortuitous however, that they had relocated to the racecourse airstrip from Ratmalana airport just over a week before the Japanese threat developed. Had they remained at Ratmalana, it is almost certain the Japanese pilots would have spotted and destroyed them.

The balance of British and Japanese aircraft was almost farcical whichever way you look at it and Churchill even asked the Admiralty why the Japanese carriers had so many more aircraft than we did. There was, of course, no stock answer to this. It was simply due to the change in Japanese fighting tactics.

During the Operation we had lost three of our largest and most important ships, the cruisers *Cornwall* and *Dorsetshire*, and the aircraft carrier *Hermes*, as well as the destroyer *Vampire*. Churchill pressed the Admiralty for Somerville's justification for sending the cruisers back to Colombo, and the *Hermes* and *Vampire* back to Trincomalee. He further questioned whether it made sense to order these ships to set sail once an air attack was expected. The Admiralty did not consider Somerville to be open to criticism for what he did at the time and said it would be unfair to assess his actions on what they knew now. Remember, Admiral Somerville only knew of the unfolding events on an hour by hour basis. It was an Operation that was taking place over an area of thousands of miles of ocean and much of the information Somerville received was second- and sometimes third-hand knowledge. It had been a game of cat and mouse. However, the loss of these four ships was firmly attributed to Somerville who had been told 'not to stick his neck out' and the blame was placed firmly on his shoulders by the Admiralty. It was the one major decision Somerville alone had made.

It raises the question, could the Eastern Fleet have done more than it did? The simple answer might be we would have fared much better had we done far less but exactly how much less could we have done? In all seriousness, the fleet could never have been given such an order but in retrospect, had they been told to keep out of the way and to stay in the western Indian Ocean, more as a deterrent force than an aggressor, the results of Japan's attacks would have had less impact. Vice-Admiral Ozawa's Malaya Force would have done neither no more nor no less than they actually did, but at least we would not have lost our two cruisers, the aircraft carrier and the destroyer, which were Ozawa's major successes.

Throughout, Admiral Somerville was staunchly supported by the First Lord of the Admiralty, Sir Dudley Pound but despite this he still had to answer for his actions. It is clear that Somerville had done his best to obey his orders and comply with the ever-changing demands of the Chiefs of Staff Committee, using a fleet whose composition was not really fit for purpose but the best that could be assembled at the time. In the course of just ten days his orders had changed from aggressive intent to full flight and a complete abandonment of all initiative in the Indian Ocean. In supporting Somerville, the Admiralty considered it had been the right decision to move the *Hermes* and the *Vampire* when he did so and it was purely bad luck that a Japanese aircraft spotted them, even though they were well clear of Trincomalee.

In retrospect much of the deficiencies of this Operation seem to stem from archaic Admiralty policies drawn up in the years between the wars. Even though the British had been pioneers in the development of the aircraft carrier, there was still an underlying preference for battleships with big guns. These die-hard Sea Lords simply could not see the immense potential striking power of naval aircraft. Resources that should have been channelled into building up the Fleet Air Arm and fitting anti-aircraft armament on our ships went instead towards building and maintaining battleships which could neither stand up to an enemy battleship – as was shown by the sinking of *HMS Hood* by a few well-placed salvoes from the *Bismarck* – or survive a well-directed air attack as the fate of *HMS Prince of Wales* had proved.

Some might argue that Somerville avoided an engagement with a vastly superior enemy force as a way of protecting the Eastern Fleet and it must have been uppermost in his mind that a prudent but ineffective Eastern Fleet in being, was of far greater value than a courageous one at the bottom of the ocean. There is no doubt that when Admiral Somerville was appointed C-in-C of the Eastern Fleet he was fully aware of the implications of the job he faced and was probably even more acutely aware of the inadequacies of the fleet he was given to command. Conversely, bearing in mind that Nagumo's express orders were to locate and destroy the British Eastern Fleet, it seems astonishing that regardless of whether it was his intention or not, Somerville's main force was never located by the Japanese. In his book *Admiral of the Pacific, the Life of Yamamoto* John Deane Potter tells how for three days the five Japanese carriers with their escorting battleships and cruisers deliberately let themselves be seen by the RAF reconnaissance planes. Nagumo hoped this would entice Somerville's fleet into a decisive daylight battle. But Somerville did not take the bait. He knew the odds were heavily against him. What he wanted was a night surface attack action.

Other accounts suggest that Somerville was in reality desperately searching for the Japanese fleet, but few accounts agree with all the known facts. Given the vastness of the Indian Ocean, it was always bound to be a game of hit-or-miss whether the two fleets would ever meet up.

Was Somerville the best man for such a crucial job? Just before the outbreak of war he had retired as being unfit for further active service and was of an age when he should have been enjoying his retirement. But in times of war few were exempt from being called up. Somerville was, in the eyes of the Admiralty, the best man for this new job. He had considerable wartime experience in the tactical operation of carrier aircraft as part of a naval force and knew the limitations of the Swordfish, the Albacore and the Fulmar aircraft but despite this, even he could not have known how greatly superior the performance of the Japanese aircraft and their elite crews were. To add to his difficulties the fleet he was given was brought together from all parts of the world and had had no time to work together, practicing the procedures involved in manoeuvring such a large number of ships. The four 'R' – class battleships were more of a handicap than an asset as they could barely make a top speed of 18 knots, a speed at which their fuel would only last for three or four days. They had to be defended against both submarine and air attack which shows they ought to have accompanied the *Warspite* and the carriers, but on the other hand their slow speed would have put the fleet at risk.

If the strategic objective was to defend Ceylon against a seaborne attack or invasion, then Admiral Somerville did not have a force capable of seeking out and successfully engaging a main Japanese battle fleet. Some high-ranking officers at the Admiralty, having been overly impressed with the exploits of torpedo armed Swordfish aircraft at Taranto and on their attack on the *Bismarck*, thought otherwise.

It meant that Ceylon would have to rely on its shore-based aircraft for its defence where like Singapore this was totally inadequate even though Admiral Sir Geoffrey Layton, C-in-C of Ceylon had greatly improved the position by diverting two Hurricane squadrons from Java. Ceylon covers an area of 250 miles by 150 miles and the air forces had to cover both Colombo and Trincomalee, each some 150 miles apart. There was no way of knowing whether or not they would come under simultaneous attack. Somerville was unaware the Japanese ships were not yet fitted with early warning radar and were unable to direct their fighters to meet an attack.

Of all the options open to the Japanese High Command, Somerville judged a sortie into the Indian Ocean was the most likely and in this event he advised the Admiralty, his strategy would be "to keep the Eastern Fleet in being and avoid losses by attrition". This was to be achieved "by keeping the fleet at sea as much as possible; to avoid it being caught in harbour; to avoid a daylight action whilst seeking to deliver night torpedo attacks; and not to undertake operations that do not give reasonable prospects of success".

It must have seemed a gloomy prospect as Somerville arrived in Colombo. His flagship *Warspite* was the only ship with suitable accommodation for all his staff. She had been launched in 1915 and had seen war service at Jutland, but since then she had been modernized and was capable of steaming at 24 knots. After only four days Somerville received his first warning of the impending Japanese attack and he did not hesitate in making plans to engage the enemy.

As planned, the fleet put to sea but from his experience Somerville knew that daylight attacks with Albacores would be both suicidal and ineffective. He felt the only strategy with these inadequate aircraft would be to make night torpedo attacks, taking advantage of the full moon on 1st April. He strongly believed that the Japanese disliked night actions and would go to almost any lengths to avoid them, a fallacy later disproved when the Japanese took on the Americans in the South Pacific. During the hours of daylight the plan was to withdraw to a position outside the enemy's air search area. For this strategy to work it was essential the enemy fleet was located and its position fixed as early as possible.

Part of Somerville's plan was thwarted by the fact we did not know exactly when to expect the Japanese attack on Ceylon. Somerville had been at sea for several days exercising his new fleet and it was time to replenish water and fuel supplies. He headed for Addu Atoll rather than Colombo because if the Japanese had attacked then, it would be a second Pearl Harbour for sure. Seldom can a fleet have been caught more on the wrong foot than Somerville was. He was 600 miles away as the first wave of Japanese aircraft struck at Ceylon. The fleet could not be brought into action either before or during the attack.

Ever since leaving Colombo, Somerville had deliberately fostered the myth of the confident imperturbable Admiral. The fact that a British fleet was avoiding contact with the enemy had to appear to be normal strategy with nothing shameful about it if morale was to be kept high. This strategy must have worked for the Eastern Fleet was saved, largely by luck. Churchill's nightmare of "the most dangerous moment of the war" had passed.

Whilst much criticism has been levelled at Admiral Somerville, to his credit he would not entertain any such criticism of the RAF or the suggestion of insufficient liaison between the two services. He could not praise the RAF enough for having acquitted themselves so well, given what little they had. It could be said that liaison between the two services was not always as close as it should have been but it must be remembered that Ceylon had not been considered as a possible theatre of war before the Japanese made their threat. Its defences were hastily thrown together and had hardly enough time to get organized before the first aircraft were upon them. Even the airfields lacked the usual organization which both aircrews and ground staff had become accustomed to at their home stations.

Someone else who played a crucial role in this campaign was Squadron Leader Leonard Birchall who is credited with having discovered the location of Vice-Admiral Nagumo's force on 4th April 1942. 413 Squadron's online history suggests Birchall "is credited with saving the island," and a Sri Lankan writer claims that 5th April 1942 was "the day Ceylon escaped Japanese occupation." Leslie Robert's history of the RCAF, *There Shall be Wings,* claims, "A single Canadian Catalina and its crew... averted a second Pearl Harbour."

But it is not true that Birchall saved Ceylon from occupation, the reason being that the Japanese had no intention of invading it at that time. The attack was simply just a raid, searching for the Eastern Fleet. The claim that Birchall prevented a second Pearl Harbour is closer to the truth, even though the bulk of the Eastern Fleet, the main Japanese target, was at Addu Atoll and not Colombo. His sighting report permitted *Cornwall* and *Dorsetshire* to manoeuvre before the attack, but miscalculation and under-estimation of Japanese aircraft performance led to their loss all the same. The same problems, and the lack of radar, led to most of the fighters defending Colombo being caught on the ground, but his warning gave 25 merchant ships sufficient time to leave Colombo harbour and get away. It also gave Somerville the chance to leave Addu Atoll eight hours before Colombo was attacked, giving him a chance to launch an air attack on Nagumo's fleet during the night of 5–6th April but just as night fell, a false report sent him haring off in the wrong direction.

It is often said it was Churchill who dubbed Birchall the 'Saviour of Ceylon,' but *The Official History of the RCAF, Volume 3,* an authoritative source, acknowledges that this label was bestowed by the Canadian press.

However, Churchill did say that Birchall "had made one of the most important single contributions to victory," but this was in 1946 when the British still thought they had destroyed more than 50 of Nagumo's aircraft, and that Japan had contemplated invasion. He did not repeat this compliment in his war memoirs, penned in *c.*1950. Indeed, Birchall was not even named and his aircraft was described simply as "a Catalina."

In hindsight, Birchall did everything he is said to have done and certainly deserves all the recognition and honours he received for it. However, it is argued that his sighting report did not result in Ceylon being saved, so strictly speaking, it is not historically accurate to call him the 'Saviour of Ceylon' but there is no doubt that he will always be the 'Saviour of Ceylon' in the eyes of many people.

From a Japanese perspective when writing his book *Zero. The Story of the Japanese Navy Air Force, 1937–45* with Jiro Horikoshi and Martin Caidin in 1957, Masatake Okumiya referred to a conversation he had had with Lieut-Commander Egusa shortly after the end of the Indian Ocean Operation. The two men were close friends, having been classmates at both the Japanese Naval Academy and later at the Navy Flying School where both became senior dive-bomber pilots. Okumiya asked Egusa how his aircraft had managed to sink so many British warships. Egusa simply shrugged his shoulders and said 'It was much simpler than bombing the *Settsu*. That's all.' The *Settsu* was Japan's old practice target battleship.

Undoubtedly it was the Zero fighter aircraft with its superior performance that made such an enormous contribution to Japan's successes. Okumiya conceded however, that except in the battle in which the Japanese torpedo and level bombers destroyed the *Prince of Wales* and the *Repulse*, the Japanese bombers were able to cause such havoc only because the Zero had won control of the air. The Zero had become the symbol of not only the Japanese land- and sea-based air power but of the entire Japanese military.

Vice-Admiral Nagumo's brief had been clear and specific – destroy the American Fleet at Pearl Harbour then drive the British Eastern Fleet out of the Indian Ocean and back to East Africa. Yes, he had destroyed the American fleet and through his attacks on Trincomalee and Colombo he had made these ports untenable. The British had made a 'tactical withdraw' so yes, Nagumo was successful in both parts of his orders. However, having determined that the British fleet would be about 100 to 150 miles from Ceylon, Nagumo ordered his reconnaissance aircraft to strenuously search this area and it is likely that the south-westerly course on which the *Dorsetshire* and the *Cornwall* were found when they were sunk may have been seen by the Japanese as their withdrawal from Ceylon. Had the Japanese investigated in greater detail and protracted the course, they would inevitably have come across the very ships they were looking for.

More than this, the sortie demonstrated Japanese superiority in carrier operations, and exposed the unprofessional manner in which the RAF was run in the East, but it did not destroy British naval power in the Indian Ocean. It is arguable that, by making full use of signal intercepts, decryption, reconnaissance and superior radar, Somerville was able to save his fast carriers *HMS Indomitable* and *Formidable* to fight another day. However, it might equally be said that the blunders made by the Royal Navy meant that the main fleet from Addu Atoll was not able to make contact with Nagumo's force as it intended.

An invasion of Ceylon was feared by the British who interpreted the Japanese failure to do so as being due to their heavy losses over Ceylon and this led to claims of a British victory. In reality the Japanese did not have the necessary men, shipping or land-based air power to spare for an invasion and occupation, and were not even in a position to make a temporary occupation. In fact, the island did not face a real threat of invasion at any point during the war.

What the raid had achieved was that it had allowed the Imperial Japanese Navy to demonstrate their superiority in the Indian Ocean and Bay of Bengal and their ability to seize territory by capturing the Andaman Islands. Despite losses, the British fleet escaped conflict by retiring but in view of the overwhelming superiority of the Japanese, particularly in carrier operations, this seems to have been a wise decision by Admiral Somerville. Japanese plans were already in place for a submarine base on the island of Madagascar from which to attack Allied shipping routes; now a weakened Ceylon invited invasion, possibly with limited objectives, like taking Trincomalee, a more convenient base.

That the British expected invasion is borne out by a speech made by Admiral Sir Geoffrey Layton, the commander of Ceylon, in mid-April to personnel of the damaged airfield at China Bay in Trincomalee harbour when he warned them, "The Japanese Fleet has retired to Singapore, to refuel and rearm, and to organise an invasion force, which we think is coming back to attack us." He ended by saying, "I am going for reinforcements, while you men here must be prepared to fight to the last man to stop the Japanese." The Admiral's speech had a negative effect on personnel, particularly his reference to leaving the island for reinforcements; afterwards he became known as "Runaway Layton".

Whereas much of the blame for the events that took place in and around Ceylon in April 1942 were attributed to Admiral Somerville, there were underlying mutterings starting to be heard at a much higher level and Churchill's future as a political leader hung in the balance. In January, Churchill had swept aside a vote of no confidence which was seen as a carefully staged demonstration of national disapproval, but throughout May and early June there were a number of events that took place in the House of Commons which collectively explain why when looking back over the war, Churchill should have deemed the Japanese Indian Ocean operation so crucial. A further motion of no confidence in the Prime Minister was introduced into the House of Commons, this time by Sir John Wardlaw-Milne, a Conservative and chairman of the All-Party Parliamentary Finance Committee. The purpose of the motion was to take not so much the central direction of the war away from Churchill, but to formulate a strategy in which as Minister of Defence he had taken a large and sometimes overriding role which it was felt should have been left to the Service Chiefs. Had the motion succeeded Churchill would have been obliged to resign as Prime Minister, but it did not. Ceylon was but one of many defeats the Allies were now facing.

Meanwhile, Japanese propaganda had an effect on much of the native population, who now awaited their arrival. Instead three British army divisions came to strengthen Ceylon's defences against a possible internal anti-British uprising and measures were implemented to improve morale, like ensuring the civilians' food rations were increased. Several minor mutinies against the British by native soldiers were quickly put down. Admiral Layton remained in Ceylon for most of the war and later, Ceylon would become an important base for the planned retaking of Malaya and Singapore.

On the whole, Ceylon benefited from its role in World War II. The plantation sector was busy meeting the urgent demands of the Allies for essential products, especially rubber, enabling the country to save a surplus in hard currency. Because the island was the seat of the Southeast Asia Command, a broad infrastructure of health services and modern amenities was built to accommodate the large number of troops posted into all parts of the country. The inherited infrastructure considerably improved the standard of living in post-war, independent Ceylon. In direct contrast, in India its nationalists demanded a guarantee of independence as recompense for their support in the war effort, whereas Ceylon committed itself wholeheartedly to the Allied war effort. Although the island was put under military jurisdiction during the war, the British and the Ceylonese maintained co-operative relations. Ceylonese pressure for political reform continued during the war, however, and increased as the Japanese threat receded and the war neared its end. The British eventually promised full participatory government once the war was at an end.

A poem written by Emlyn Parry, a former seaman of *HMS Dorsetshire* who died in the 1960s as a result of his injuries.

Come with me awhile, and see a ship in gallant style,
Floundered by an enemy hand, posing for her final stand.
Burning not from heat of sun, but from the enemy and his gun.
Catch the devils that fly so low, empty their greed on decks below.
Load the guns, though flounder she may, or you'll never fight another day.
Watch her stagger with broken spine, with those who are left with guns
in line.
Backs to the wall with sweat on the brow, before she makes her final bow.
Blood on the body, eyes to the sky, they're not ready to let her die.
Strong an arm that loads a gun, stronger the heart of a mother's son.
Come closer, watch the flesh apart, but closer still, no breaking heart.
The politicians' arena takes its toll, and a sailor's foot seldom treads the soil.
See her structure with cautious eye, stripped like a tree when locusts fly.
Take heed of broken bodies there, laddered fathoms take them to care.
No mothers' arms to hold their own, but salt of sea will wash their bones.
Clasp tight your hand she's listing now, the water laps the starboard bow.
She quivers now, this lady fine, ripped apart, her beauteous line.
No foe to strike, no guns to hear, no bosun at the wheel to steer.
No siren now from her lofty heights, only a shredded ensign flights.
Watch with me while battle ends, heartbreaks that a nation sends.
See the shore that lies o'er there, ten thousand miles to a mother's despair.
Watch the horror, and never to learn, a tear on the cheek and a no return.
Think of a chair forever empty t'will be, but a mighty heart fought well
at sea.
Step back apace and watch her go, to rest her back well down below.
Gaze awhile and watch the sea where fought a crew for you and me.
See man's blood mix with the deep, hells' struggle there to darkness seep.
Trespass your heart and close your eyes, for a sailor's hope and his ship
that dies.

Further Reading

Agar VC, RN, Capt. Augustus, *Footprints in the Sea*. Evans 1900.

Birchall RCAF, Leonard & Paterson, Michael, *Battle for the Skies*. David & Charles, 2004.

Bryant, Arthur, *The Turn of the Tide*. Doubleday 1957.

Dull, Paul S., *A Battle History of the Imperial Japanese Navy 1941–45*. Patrick Stephens Ltd 1978.

Kitchen, Geoff, *An account of the loss of HMS Dorsetshire in the Indian Ocean, Easter Day, 5th April 1942*. An unpublished book.

Lowry, Thomas P & Wellham, John W.G., *The Attack on Taranto: Blueprint for Pearl Harbor*. Stackpole Books 1995.

MacIntyre, Capt. Donald, *The Fighting Admiral*. Evans Brothers Limited 1961.

Okumiya, Masatake, Horikoshi, Jiro and Caidin, Martin, *Zero. The Story of the Japanese Navy Air Force, 1937–45*. Cassell and Co. Ltd, 1957.

Potter, John Deane, *Admiral of the Pacific, the Life of Yamamoto*. Heinemann 1965.

Pugsley, Rear Admiral A.F., *Destroyer Man*. Weidenfeld and Nicholson 1957.

Tomlinson, Michael, *The Most Dangerous Moment*. Granada Publishing Ltd. 1979.

Wallace, Gordon, *Carrier Observer*. Airlife Publishing Ltd. 1993.

Index

L77,L9